STRINGING  ALONG

WITH VANESSA-ANN

That Patchwork Place®

Trice Boerens

Acknowledgments

The Vanessa-Ann Collection

Owner: Jo Packham

Designer: Trice Boerens

Editor-in-Chief/Technical Editor ...... Barbara Weiland
Technical/Copy Editor .... Sharon Rose
Managing Editor .... Greg Sharp
Typesetting, Illustrations
   and Graphic Design .... Petersen Communications
Photography .... Ryne Hazen
Photo Stylist .... Jo Packham
Cover Photography .... Brent Kane
Cover Photo Stylist .... Susan I. Jones

Stringing Along
©1995 by That Patchwork Place, Inc.,
P.O. Box 118
Bothell, WA 98041-0118
USA

Printed in Hong Kong
00 99 98 97 96 95   6 5 4 3 2 1

MISSION STATEMENT

WE ARE DEDICATED TO PROVIDING QUALITY PRODUCTS THAT ENCOURAGE CREATIVITY AND PROMOTE SELF-ESTEEM IN OUR CUSTOMERS AND OUR EMPLOYEES.

WE STRIVE TO MAKE A DIFFERENCE IN THE LIVES WE TOUCH.

That Patchwork Place is an employee-owned, financially secure company.

Contents

String Piecing

Snips and bits from the scrap bag, odd lots, remnants and impulse purchases put away "for later"—these are the stored treasures of those who love to quilt. Happily, these are also the perfect fabrics for string piecing, the subject of this book!

String piecing was born of necessity. In older times, frugality demanded that every scrap of fabric, whatever its color, be saved and used. Even with all the fabrics available today, string quilts retain their cozy charm and simplicity. Complex-appearing striped blocks, diamonds, triangles, checkerboard borders and other shapes are easily created by piecing fabric strips together.

The quilts in this book combine string-pieced blocks with appliquéd designs. Some are embellished with ribbon and buttons. Some tell a story, and some are delightful, eye-fooling geometric designs.

Try your own color and print combinations to make each one uniquely your own. Experiment with different textures of fabric—velvet, silk, rough tweeds, wool, brocades—the choices are endless!

Once the quilt top is pieced and assembled, all that remains is to baste it together with the lining, batting and backing, then quilt away. Bind the edges and you're ready to show off a beautiful family heirloom-to-be.

Portions of the designs shown may also be used for pillow tops, place mats, pot holders and oven mitts, table cloths, chair cushions, fabric frames for favorite photographs, vests, tote bags and more.

Each project in this book includes detailed diagrams and full-size templates to help you put your quilt together. All measurements and piecing templates include $1/4$"-wide seam allowances. Basic quiltmaking techniques are covered in the General Directions, beginning on page 90.

So get out the scrap bag and let's quilt!

About the Designer

Trice Boerens lives and works at the foot of Mount Ogden in Ogden, Utah. She has been a quilter for many years, combining her designing with the raising of two boys and two girls.

Quilting, stenciling, painting, cross-stitchery, scrap crafts—Trice's home displays many of her talents, plus a wonderful collection of teddy bears that even includes an astronaut-bear.

For this book, Trice designed and stitched every quilt, putting her unique signature on each one. She hopes that all of you will have as much fun with these projects as she did.

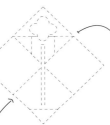

Shades of Lavender

Finished Size: 50" x 62"
Finished Block Size: 4$\frac{1}{4}$" x 4$\frac{1}{4}$"

Materials (44"-wide fabric)	**Cutting** (Use templates on pages 9-10.)
$\frac{3}{8}$ yd. each of 5 coordinating prints in shades of mauve, lavender, and gray/blue	See cutting information in directions for "Pieced Blocks" and "Pieced Sashing" on page 7.
$\frac{3}{4}$ yd. white-on-white print for plain and pieced blocks	18 squares, each 4$\frac{3}{4}$" x 4$\frac{3}{4}$" (or use Template A) 6 Template C 6 Template D
3$\frac{3}{4}$ yds. light green for backing* and triangles	2 pieces, each 33" x 55"* 12 Template B 24 Template C 6 Template F
1$\frac{1}{4}$ yd. blue/green print for flowers	6 Template H 6 Template G 12 Template E 6 strips, each 1" x 6", for stems
1$\frac{1}{2}$ yds. lavender paisley print**	2 strips, each 7$\frac{1}{4}$" x 48$\frac{1}{2}$", for side borders 2 strips, each 7$\frac{1}{4}$" x 50", for top and bottom borders 12 strips, each 1" x 9$\frac{1}{2}$", for pieced sashing
$\frac{1}{4}$ yd. lavender solid	See cutting information in directions for "Pieced Sashing" on page 7.
$\frac{1}{4}$ yd. light blue solid	See cutting information in directions for "Pieced Sashing" on page 7.
$\frac{3}{8}$ yd. gray/blue solid for sashing	3 strips, each 2" x 36$\frac{1}{2}$"
$\frac{5}{8}$ yd. lilac print for binding	6$\frac{1}{2}$ yds. of 2"-wide bias strips
53" x 65" piece of batting White thread for quilting	

* Cut the large pieces for the backing first and set aside. Cut the remaining pieces from the leftover yardage.

** Cut the border strips first, from the length of the fabric, and set aside. Cut the remaining pieces from the leftover strip.

Directions

All seam allowances are ¼" wide.

Pieced Blocks

1. From the 5 coordinating print fabrics, cut a total of 90 strips, each 21" long and varying in width from ³/₄" to 1¹/₂". Alternating colors and widths, sew strips together along the long edges to create 6 different string-pieced units, each measuring 21" long and at least 7" wide. Set aside leftover strips for "Pieced Sashing."

   From each string-pieced unit, cut 3 Template A, aligning the grain-line arrow in the center of the block with a seam line in the unit (Diagram 1). You need a total of 18 string-pieced squares.

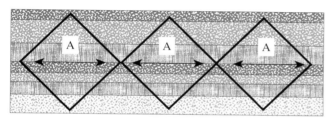

Diagram 1

2. Make 9 Four-Patch blocks, using 2 string-pieced squares and 2 white-on-white 4³/₄" squares (Diagram 2).

Diagram 2

3. Make 6 Flower Blocks, using white-on-white Pieces C and D and blue/green Piece E (Diagram 3). Press center seam toward the E in E/D/E.

Diagram 3

4. Make 6 Flower Pot Blocks, using light green Pieces F and blue/green Pieces G (Diagram 4). Press the seam toward Piece G.

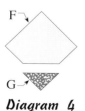

Diagram 4

5. To complete each Flower Block unit, sew a light green Piece C to adjacent top edges (Diagram 5). To complete each Flower Pot unit, sew a light green Piece C to the adjacent bottom edges (Diagram 6).

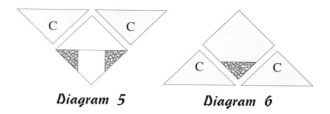

Diagram 5   **Diagram 6**

6. Arrange the completed blocks and units in 3 identical horizontal rows as shown. Sew the blocks and units together in diagonal rows, then sew the rows together, adding light green Piece B to the upper left and lower right corners of each strip last. You should have 3 strips, each 12¹/₂" x 36¹/₂" (Diagram 7).

7. Appliqué 1 flower and 1 stem to each Flower/Flower Pot unit (Diagram 8). Set the 3 completed Flower Pot strips aside. See "Applique" on page 91.

Diagram 8

Pieced Sashing

1. From the solid-colored lavender, cut strips 9¹/₂" long and varying in width from 2¹/₂" to 3". From the solid-colored light blue, cut strips 9¹/₂" long and varying in width from 1" to 1¹/₂".

2. Cut 9¹/₂"-long pieces from the remaining print strips.

Diagram 7

3. Alternating fabrics and widths, sew these strips, the strips cut in step 1 above, and the 1" x 9½" lavender paisley print strips together along the long edges to make 3 string-pieced units that are each at least 12½" long. Cut each string-pieced unit into 3 strips, each 3" x 12½" (Diagram 9).

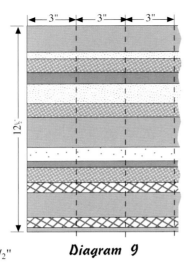

Diagram 9

4. Sew 3 string-pieced units together short end to short end. Resulting size should be 3" x 36½". Repeat to make 3 pieced sashing strips.

5. Sew the bottom of a Flower Pot strip to the top edge of a gray/blue sashing strip. Sew a pieced sashing strip to the bottom edge of the gray/blue strip. Repeat with remaining strips.

Quilt Top Assembly

Refer to Diagram 10.

1. Sew the Flower Pot/Sashing units together to complete the center of the quilt top.

2. Sew the 7¼" x 48½" lavender paisley strips to the long sides of the quilt top. Sew the 7¼" x 50" lavender paisley border strips to the top and bottom of the quilt top.

Finishing

Refer to pages 94-96 in "General Directions."

1. To prepare the backing, sew the 55" x 33" pale green backing strips together along the 55" edge. Press seams open.

2. Mark quilting lines at the center of each fabric used in diamond string-pieced sections, parallel with the seams. Mark vertical lines in each solid fabric of pieced sashing. Mark remaining quilting lines shown in Diagram 11.

3. Layer the quilt top with batting and backing; baste.

4. Quilt by hand or machine, using white thread.

5. Bind the edges with lilac double-layer bias binding.

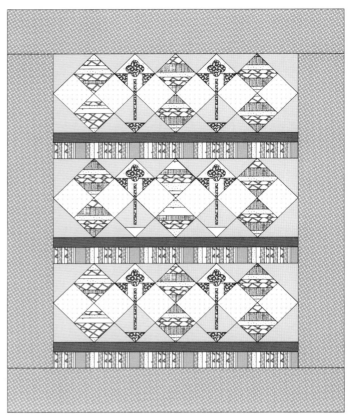

Diagram 10

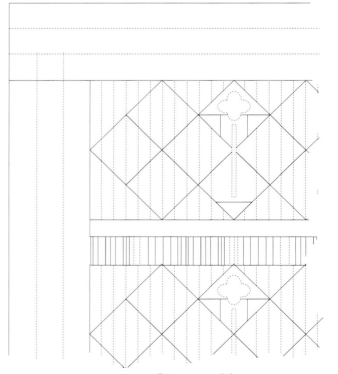

Diagram 11
Upper-left corner of quilt

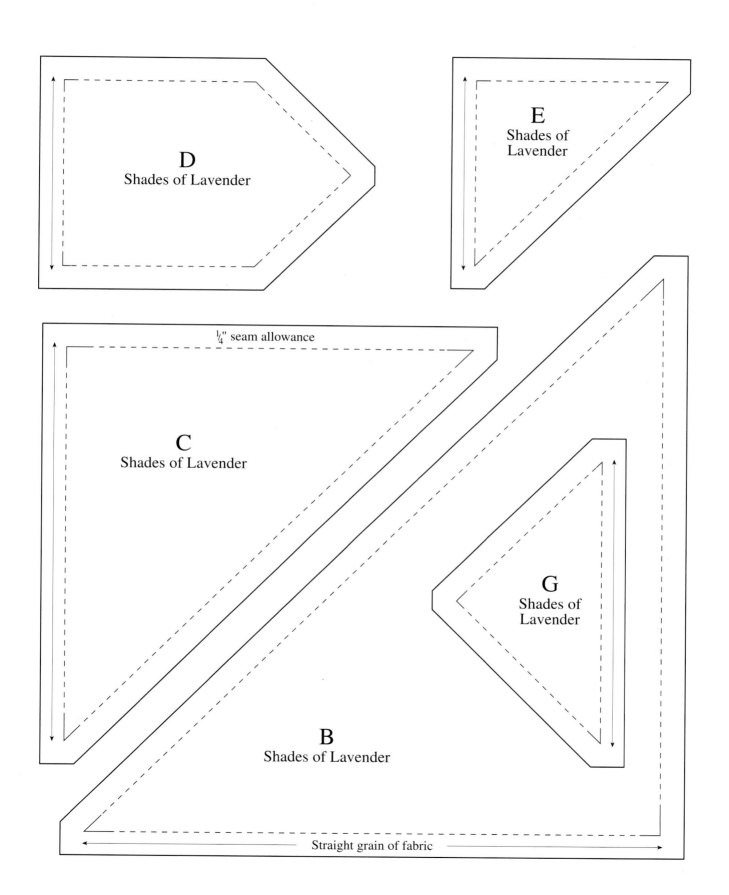

D
Shades of Lavender

E
Shades of
Lavender

¼" seam allowance

C
Shades of Lavender

G
Shades of
Lavender

B
Shades of Lavender

Straight grain of fabric

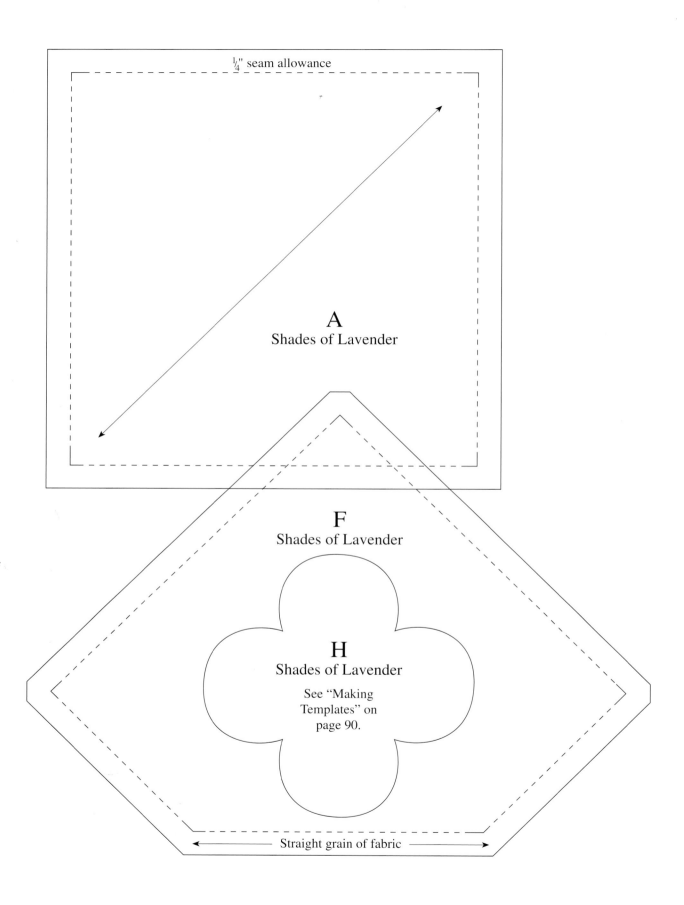

¼" seam allowance

A
Shades of Lavender

F
Shades of Lavender

H
Shades of Lavender

See "Making
Templates" on
page 90.

Straight grain of fabric

Heart Strings

Finished Size: 32$\frac{1}{2}$" x 42$\frac{1}{2}$"
Finished Block Size: 8" x 9"

Materials *(44"-wide fabric)*	Cutting *(Use templates on page 17.)*
3 yds. pink roses print for Heart blocks, pieced borders, lower inner border, and quilt backing	1 piece, 36" x 46", for quilt backing 1 strip, 1" x 22", (heart strip) 1 strip, 7$\frac{1}{2}$" x 24$\frac{1}{2}$", for lower inner border 9 rectangles, each 8$\frac{1}{2}$" x 9$\frac{1}{2}$" 2 strips, each 2$\frac{1}{2}$" x 42" 1 strip, 2$\frac{1}{2}$" x 11"
2 yds. burgundy/blue print for binding, pieced border, and heart strips	4$\frac{3}{8}$ yds. of 1$\frac{1}{2}$"-wide bias strips 2 strips, each 2$\frac{1}{2}$" x 42" See additional cutting information in directions for "Heart Blocks" on page 13.
$\frac{1}{4}$ yd. cream/pink print for pieced border	2 strips, each 2$\frac{1}{2}$" x 42" 1 strip, 2$\frac{1}{2}$" x 11"
$\frac{1}{2}$ yd. pink solid for pieced border	2 strips, each 2$\frac{1}{2}$" x 42"
$\frac{1}{4}$ yd. red/white floral print for heart strips	See cutting information in directions for "Heart Blocks" on page 13.
$\frac{1}{8}$ yd. dusty rose print for diagonal strips in Heart blocks	1$\frac{1}{8}$ yds. total of 1$\frac{1}{2}$"-wide strips
$\frac{1}{8}$ yd. lavender paisley print for diagonal strips in Heart blocks	2$\frac{1}{2}$ yds. total of 1$\frac{1}{2}$"-wide strips
$\frac{1}{2}$ yd. cream solid for heart "lace"	9 Template B
1$\frac{5}{8}$ yds. 1$\frac{1}{2}$"-wide gold-edged rose French wire ribbon for large bow $\frac{3}{4}$ yd. 1"-wide lilac ribbon for small bow 36" x 46" piece of batting	

Directions

All seam allowances are ¼" wide.

Heart Blocks

1. From the burgundy/blue and the red/white floral fabrics, cut assorted 22"-long strips, ranging in width from ¾" to 2" wide. Sew strips together in random order to make 5 string-pieced units, each 22" long and at least 5½" wide. Incorporate the 1" x 22" strip of pink roses print into one of the units.

2. Using Template A, cut 9 half-hearts from the string-pieced units; reverse the template and cut 9 more. Line up the grain-line arrow with a seam in the string-pieced unit before cutting (Diagram 1). Arrange half-hearts in random pairs.

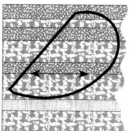

Diagram 1

3. With right sides together, sew the pairs together and press the seams open (Diagram 2).

Diagram 2

4. Center a cream ruffle (Template B) in each of the 8½" x 9½" pieces of pink roses print. Appliqué in place. See "Appliqué" on page 91.

5. Center a string-pieced heart in the center of each ruffle and appliqué in place (Diagram 3). See "Appliqué" beginning on page 91. Set 4 of the completed blocks aside.

Diagram 3

6. Add diagonal strips to the corners of the 5 remaining heart blocks. Place 1 lavender paisley or dusty rose strip across 1 corner of a heart block, right sides together. Stitch ¼" from the upper long edge (Diagram 4).

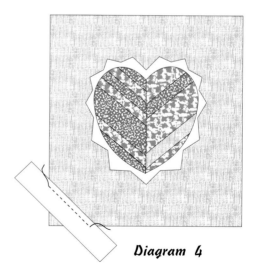

Diagram 4

Press the strip toward the block and trim excess strip even with the edges of the block. Turn under ¹/₄" along the remaining long edge of the strip and slipstitch in place (Diagram 5). Repeat on the remaining block corners, adding more than one strip on some corners and varying the angles. See the completed blocks in Diagram 10 on page 16.

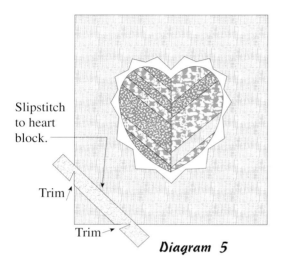

Slipstitch to heart block.

Trim

Trim

Diagram 5

Quilt Top Assembly

Refer to Diagram 10 on page 15 for the following steps.

1. Arrange the completed Heart blocks in 3 rows of 3 blocks each, placing the blocks with the diagonal strips in the corners and in the center position.

2. Sew the blocks together in rows, then sew the rows together, matching seams carefully.

3. Sew the 7¹/₂" x 24¹/₂" strip of pink roses fabric to the bottom edge of the bottom row of blocks. Set the quilt center aside.

Pieced Border

Refer to the quilt photo and Diagram 10 on page 15 for the following steps.

1. Sew a 2¹/₂" x 42" burgundy/blue strip to a 2¹/₂" x 42" pink roses print strip. Press the seam toward the darker color. Make a second strip unit with the remaining 42"-long burgundy/blue and pink roses strips. Do the same with cream/pink strips and the pink strips. Cut a total of 31 segments, each 2¹/₂" wide, from each color combination (Diagram 6).

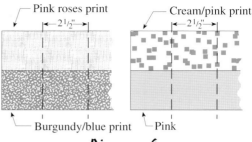

Pink roses print — 2¹/₂" — Cream/pink print — 2¹/₂"

Burgundy/blue print — Pink

Diagram 6

2. Join the segments into 15 of Four-patch Block A and 15 of Four-patch Block B (Diagram 7). Set the remaining segments aside.

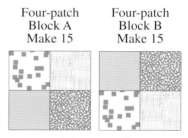

Four-patch Block A Make 15   Four-patch Block B Make 15

Diagram 7

3. For the top border, join 6 Four-patch Block A (Diagram 10 on page 16). Sew to the top edge of the quilt top with the burgundy/blue print and pink squares in each unit next to the quilt top.

4. For the bottom border, join 6 Four-patch Block B (Diagram 10 on page 16). Sew to the bottom edge of the quilt top with the burgundy/blue and pink squares next to the quilt top.

5. Sew the 2¹/₂" x 11" cream pink print strip to the 2¹/₂" x 11" pink roses print strip. Press the seam toward the darker color. Cut 4 segments each, 2¹/₂" wide, from the resulting unit (Diagram 8).

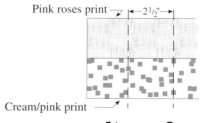

Pink roses print — 2¹/₂"

Cream/pink print

Diagram 8

6. Make the four-patch units shown in Diagram 9 using the segments set aside in step 2 and segments cut in step 5.

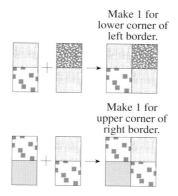

Make 1 for lower corner of left border.

Make 1 for upper corner of right border.

Diagram 9

7. Assemble the left-hand and right-hand borders, referring to Diagram 10 for block placement and using the remaining segments cut in step 5 for the upper left and lower right border corners. Sew completed borders to the quilt top, paying careful attention to color placement.

Four-patch Block A

Four-patch Block A

Four-patch Block B

Four-patch Block B

Diagram 10

Finishing

Refer to pages 94-96 in the "General Directions."

1. Mark quilting lines as shown in Diagram 11.

2. Layer the quilt top with batting and backing; baste.

3. Quilt by hand or machine.

4. Bind the edges with single-layer bias strips cut from the burgundy/blue print, rounding off the corners.

5. Embellish the bottom inner border strip. To make the bow, center the lilac ribbon on top of the rose ribbon. Handling both ribbons as one, tie a bow. Center the bow knot 2" below the top edge of the bottom inner border strip. Tack in place. Arrange the bow loops and ribbon tails as desired and tack in place, using thread to match the ribbons. (See the quilt photo and Diagram 10 on page 16.)

Diagram 11

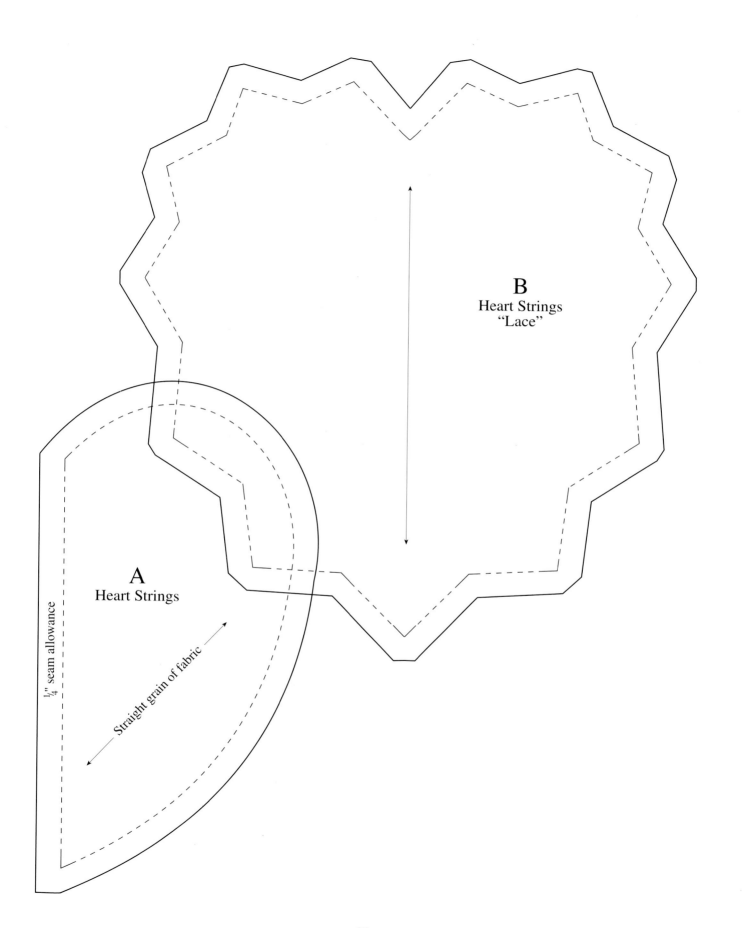

B
Heart Strings
"Lace"

A
Heart Strings

¼" seam allowance

Straight grain of fabric

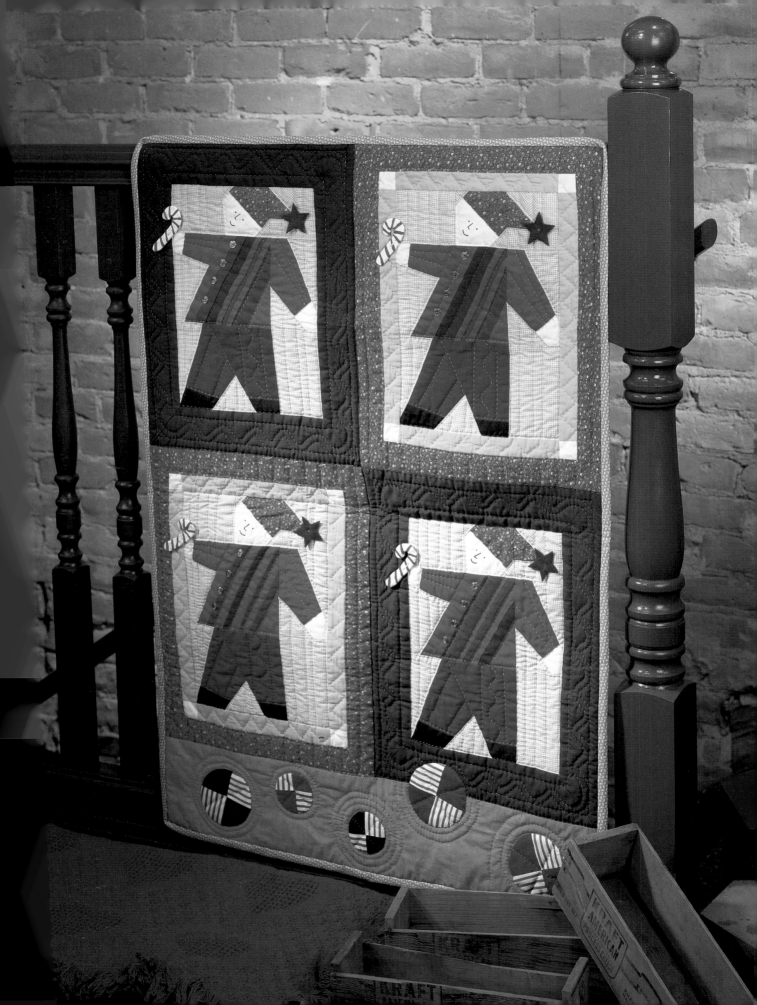

Santas on Parade

Finished Size: 28$\frac{1}{2}$" x 41$\frac{1}{2}$"
Finished Block Size: 9" x 13"

Materials (44"-wide fabric)	*Cutting* (Use templates on pages 25-28.)
1$\frac{1}{2}$ yds. light green checked fabric for block backgrounds and backing	32" x 45" piece for backing 8 Template A 4 each of Templates C, D, E, F, I, J, L, N, Q and S
$\frac{1}{2}$ yd. red fabric for blocks	4 Template H 4 Template K See additional cutting information in directions for "Santa Blocks."
$\frac{1}{4}$ yd. dark red fabric for blocks	See cutting information in directions for "Santa Blocks" on page 20.
$\frac{1}{2}$ yd. burgundy fabric for blocks and appliquéd balls	4 Template O 4 Template P 2 strips, 2$\frac{1}{2}$" x 8"; see additional cutting See additional cutting information in directions for "Pieced Circles" on pages 22-23.
$\frac{1}{4}$ yd. red print for blocks and borders	4 Template B 4 Template C 4 strips, each 2" x 16" 4 strips, each 2" x 20"
$\frac{1}{8}$ yd. white fabric for blocks	4 Template B 4 Template G 4 Template M 8 squares, each 1$\frac{1}{2}$" x 1$\frac{1}{2}$"
$\frac{1}{2}$ yd. dark green fabric for blocks and borders and appliquéd balls	4 Template R 4 Template T 4 strips, each 3" x 16" 4 strips, each 3" x 20" 2 strips, 2$\frac{1}{2}$" x 5$\frac{1}{2}$" See additional cutting information in directions for "Pieced Circles" on pages 22-23.
$\frac{1}{4}$ yd. gold fabric for sashing	4 strips, each 1$\frac{1}{2}$" x 9$\frac{1}{2}$" 4 strips, each 1$\frac{1}{2}$" x 13$\frac{1}{2}$"

(continued on page 20)

Materials *(continued)*	**Cutting** *(continued)*
¹/₄ yd. brown fabric for bottom border	1 strip, 5¹/₂" x 28¹/₂"
¹/₈ yd. olive-striped fabric for balls	2 strips, 2¹/₂" x 5¹/₂"* 2 strips, 2¹/₂" x 8"*
³/₈ yd. green print for binding	4¹/₄ yds. total of 2"-wide bias strips
32" x 45" piece of batting	
Thread White polymer clay for candy canes Paring knife for cutting clay Round toothpick Acrylic paints: red, burgundy Spray gloss varnish 4 star ornaments or buttons, each 1³/₄" diameter 16 gold buttons, ³/₈" diameter Black fine-tip, permanent marking pen	

*Cut one strip with stripes positioned vertically. Cut remaining strip with stripes positioned horizontally. (See "Pieced Circles" on page 22.)

Directions

All seam allowances are ¹/₄" wide.

Santa Blocks

1. Make faces. Sew a white Template B to a red print Template B along the long edges. Sew a green checked Template A to each short edge (Diagram 1). Make 4 faces.

2. Make hat tips. Sew a green checked Template C and a red print Template C together on the long edges. Sew a green checked Template E to the right edge of Unit C/C. Sew a green checked F to the bottom of Unit C/C/E (Diagram 2). Make 4 hat tips.

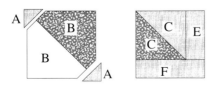

Diagram 1   *Diagram 2*

3. Assemble the top section of each Santa. Sew a green checked Template D to the left edge of each face. Sew a hat tip to the right edge of each face (Diagram 3). Set aside.

Diagram 3

4. Make jackets. From red, dark red, and burgundy fabrics, cut a total of 16 strips, each 16" long and varying in width from ³/₄" to 1¹/₂". Sew strips together on long edges, alternating fabrics as desired, to make 2 string-pieced units, each 6" x 16". Cut 4 Template W, aligning the grain-line arrow with a seam line in the pieced unit.

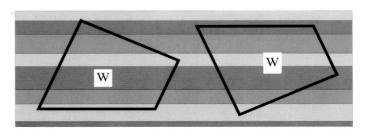

Diagram 4

5. Make left arm. Sew a white Template G to a red Template H. Then add a green checked Template I to the lower slanted edge (Diagram 5). Make 4.

6. Make right arm. Sew a white Template M to a red Template K. Add a green checked Template L to the upper slanted edge and a green checked Template J to the lower slanted edge (Diagram 6). Make 4.

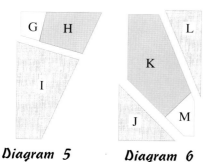

Diagram 5   **Diagram 6**

7. Assemble middle section. Sew a left and right arm to each jacket (Diagram 7).

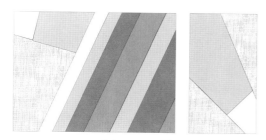

Diagram 7

8. Make left leg. Sew a dark green Template R to a burgundy Template O (Diagram 8). Then sew a green checked Template S to the right edge of the unit and a green checked Template N to the left edge, aligning bottom edges (Diagram 9). Make 4.

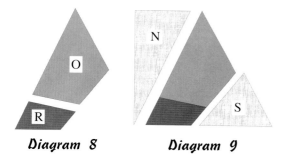

Diagram 8   **Diagram 9**

9. Make right leg. Sew a dark green Template T to a burgundy Template P (Diagram 10). Sew a green checked Template Q to the long straight edge of leg (Diagram 11). Make 4.

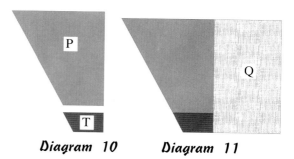

Diagram 10   **Diagram 11**

10. Assemble the bottom section. Sew left and right legs together on the slanted edge (Diagram 12). Make 4 bottom sections.

Diagram 12

11. Assemble complete figure. Sew the top, middle and bottom sections together on the long edges (Diagram 13). Make 4 figures, each measuring $9^1/_2$" x $13^1/_2$".

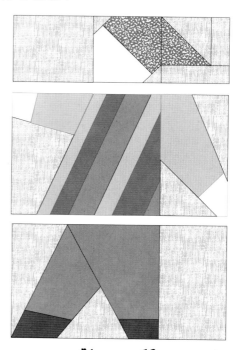

Diagram 13

Santa Blocks Assembly

1. Add borders to Santa Block 1. Sew the 3"-wide dark green borders to 2 of the pieced Santas, mitering corners as shown on page 93. Each Santa Block 1 should measure 14½" x 18½" (Diagram 14).

Diagram 14

2. Add borders to Santa Block 2. Sew a white 1½" square to each end of each of the four 1½" x 9½" gold sashing strips for a total of 4 border strips (Diagram 15).

Diagram 15

3. Sew a 1½" x 13½" gold sashing strip to each long edge of 2 pieced Santas. Then sew 1 white/gold border strip to the top and bottom edges of each one (Diagram 16).

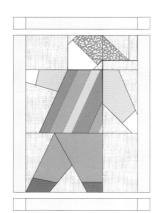

Diagram 16

4. Sew red print border strips to each Santa Block 2, mitering corners as shown on page 93. Each Santa Block 2 should now measure 14½" x 18½" (Diagram 17).

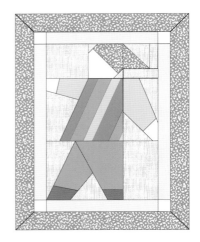

Diagram 17

Quilt Top Assembly

1. Referring to Diagram 18 on page 23, sew the completed Santa blocks together in 2 rows of 2 blocks each. Sew the rows together.

2. Sew the 5½" x 28½" strip of brown fabric to the bottom edge of the assembled blocks.

Pieced Circles

1. Sew each olive-striped 8"-long strip to one burgundy 8"-long strip. Cut into 2½"-wide strips (Diagram 19).

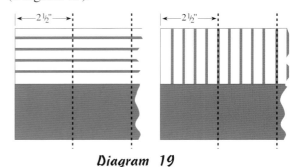

Diagram 19

2. Sew 2 of the resulting strips together into a Four-patch block as shown in Diagram 20. Repeat to make 3 burgundy Four-patch blocks.

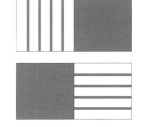

Diagram 20

Diagram 18

3. Cut 2 of Template U and 1 of Template V from the burgundy Four-patch blocks (Diagram 21).

4. Repeat Steps 1 and 2, using the 5½"-long strips of the olive-striped and dark green fabrics. Make

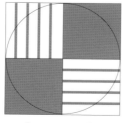

Diagram 21

2 Four-patch blocks and cut 1 of Template U and 1 of Template V.

5. Referring to the photo and Diagram 18 for placement, appliqué the pieced circles to the brown border. See "Appliqué" on page 91.

Embellishments

1. Roll polymer clay out to ¹/₈" thickness. Cut out 4 candy canes. Use toothpick to pierce a hole in the top. Bake following manufacturer's directions. Paint candy canes with red stripes. Allow to dry. Spray with two coats of varnish. Dry thoroughly.

2. Paint star ornaments burgundy. Allow to dry.

3. Referring to the photo for placement, sew 4 buttons on each Santa.

4. Referring to the face pattern on Template B, draw the features on each face with the black fine-tip, permanent marking pen.

Finishing

Refer to pages 94-96 in the "General Directions."

1. Mark quilting lines on the quilt top, referring to Diagrams 22, 23, and 24 below.

2. Layer the quilt top with batting and backing; baste.

3. Quilt by hand or machine.

4. Bind the edges with double-layer green print bias.

5. Referring to the quilt photo for placement, sew star ornaments and candy canes to each figure, stitching through all layers.

Diagram 22
Santa with Gold Border

Diagram 23
Santa with Green Border

Diagram 24
Bottom Brown Border

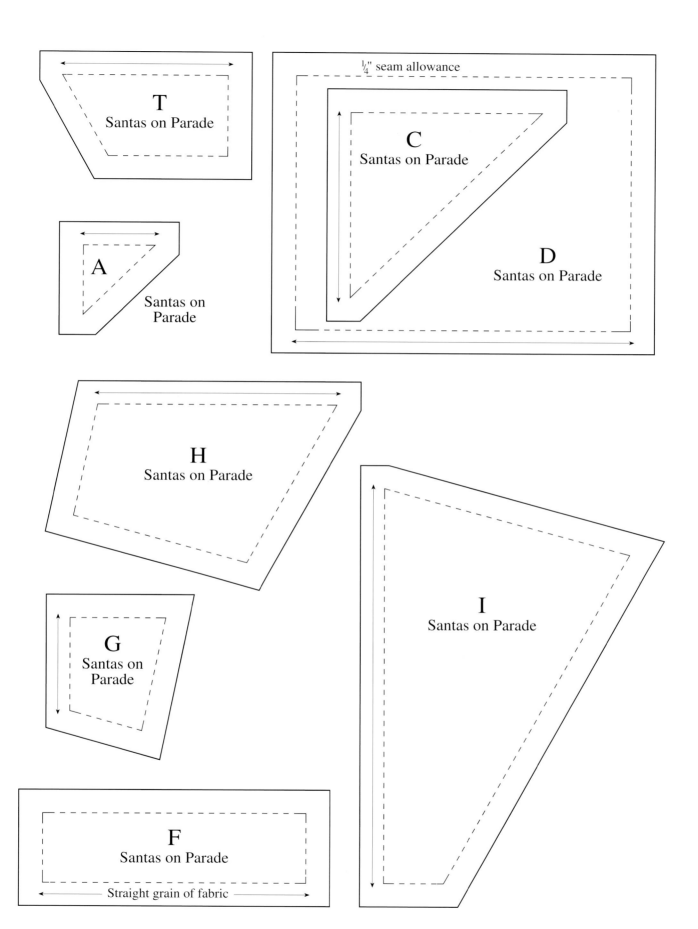

T
Santas on Parade

A
Santas on Parade

¼" seam allowance

C
Santas on Parade

D
Santas on Parade

H
Santas on Parade

I
Santas on Parade

G
Santas on Parade

F
Santas on Parade

Straight grain of fabric

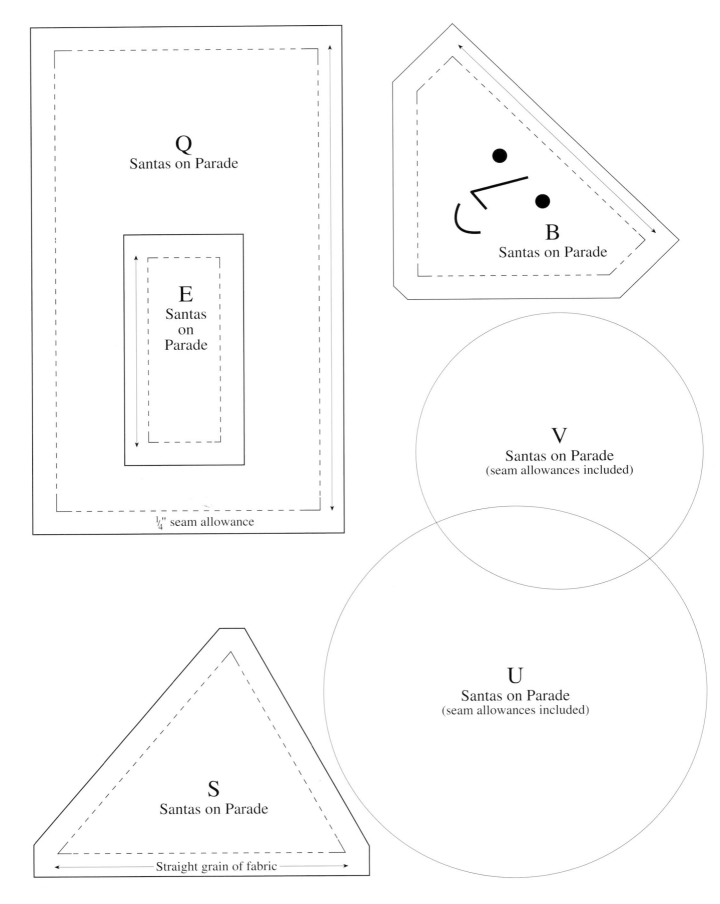

Q
Santas on Parade

E
Santas
on
Parade

¼" seam allowance

B
Santas on Parade

V
Santas on Parade
(seam allowances included)

U
Santas on Parade
(seam allowances included)

S
Santas on Parade

Straight grain of fabric

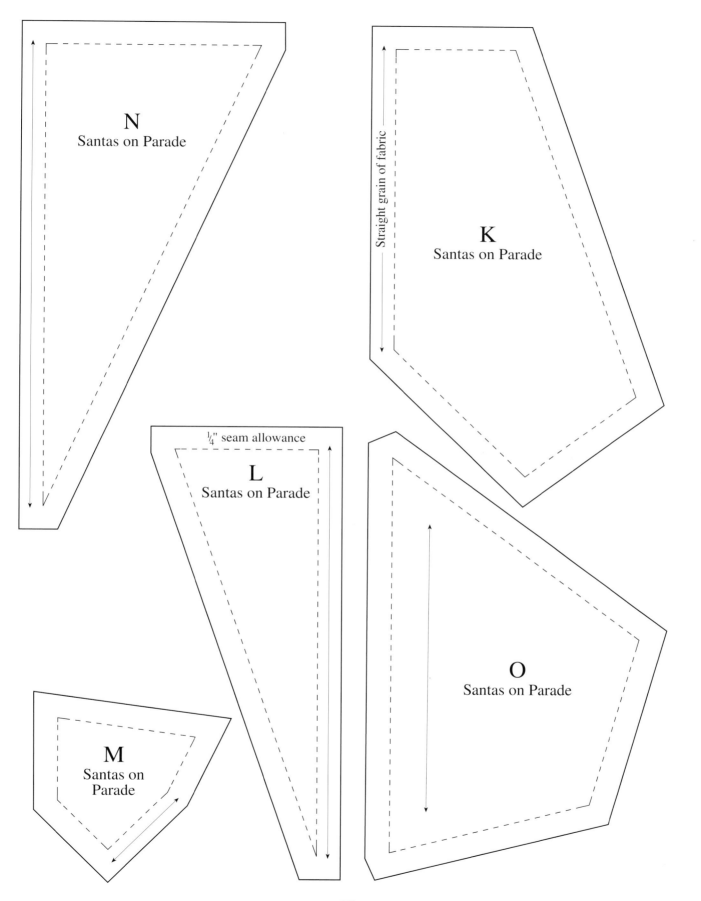

N
Santas on Parade

K
Santas on Parade

Straight grain of fabric

¼" seam allowance

L
Santas on Parade

M
Santas on Parade

O
Santas on Parade

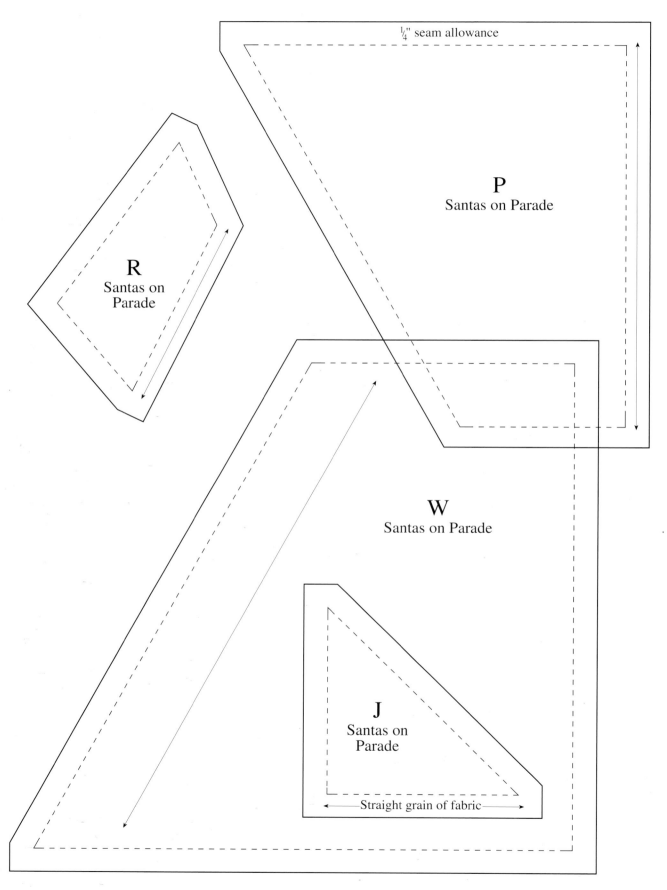

¼" seam allowance

P
Santas on Parade

R
Santas on
Parade

W
Santas on Parade

J
Santas on
Parade

Straight grain of fabric

Fancy Fans

Finished Size: 64$^{1}/_{4}$" x 64$^{1}/_{4}$"
Block Size: 5$^{1}/_{4}$" x 5$^{1}/_{4}$"

Materials (44"-wide fabric)	***Cutting*** (Use templates on page 35.)
1 yd. large floral print for Fans	41 Template B
$^{5}/_{8}$ yd. yellow/white striped fabric for fan tops	41 Template A*
$^{1}/_{4}$ yd. dark-blue paisley print for Fan Blocks	6 squares, each 5$^{3}/_{4}$" x 5$^{3}/_{4}$"
$^{3}/_{8}$ yd. tan paisley print for Fan Blocks	9 squares, each 5$^{3}/_{4}$" x 5$^{3}/_{4}$"
$^{1}/_{4}$ yd. brown/black print for Fan Blocks	7 squares, each 5$^{3}/_{4}$" x 5$^{3}/_{4}$"
$^{1}/_{4}$ yd. each of 2 different blue/green prints for Fan Blocks	7 squares, each 5$^{3}/_{4}$" x 5$^{3}/_{4}$"; cut 3 from one print and 4 from the other.
$^{1}/_{2}$ yd. tan/green floral print for Fan Blocks and Cabin Corner Blocks A-3 and B-3	12 squares, each 5$^{3}/_{4}$" x 5$^{3}/_{4}$"; set aside remainder to use in Cabin Corner Blocks.
$^{1}/_{2}$ yd. light-tan/red floral print for Cabin Corner Blocks A-3 and B-3, and corner squares	4 squares, each 7" x 7"; set aside remainder to use in Cabin Corner Blocks.
$^{1}/_{2}$ yd. dark green solid-colored fabric for inner borders	6 strips, each 2$^{1}/_{4}$" x 42"**
1$^{1}/_{8}$ yds. brown print for outer borders	5 strips, each 7" x 42"**
3 yds. blue-and-tan print for backing and binding	1 piece, 68" long and the width of the fabric 2 pieces, each 15" x 68" 7$^{1}/_{2}$ yds. total of 2"-wide bias strips
1$^{1}/_{8}$ yds. muslin for Cabin Corner Block backings	41 pieces, each 5$^{3}/_{4}$" x 5$^{3}/_{4}$"***
68" x 68" piece of batting White thread for quilting	

   * Center the template over the print to include a large flower in each one.
  ** Directions for piecing and applying 4 inner border strips and 4 outer border strips of the appropriate
      lengths appear on page 33. If the outer border fabric does not measure at least 42" wide after
      preshrinking, you will need an additional $^{1}/_{4}$ yd. of fabric so you can cut one more 7"-wide strip.
*** If muslin is less than 42" wide after preshrinking, you will need an additional $^{1}/_{4}$ yard.

(continued on page 31)

Materials *(continued)*

Use the following fabrics to string piece the Cabin Corner Blocks, along with leftovers from the above fabrics. Cutting directions follow in the Cabin Corner Block directions.

$^3/_4$ yd. cream fabric for all Cabin Corner Blocks
$^1/_2$ yd. cream/red pindot fabric for all Cabin Corner Blocks
$^1/_2$ yd. cream/blue pindot for all Cabin Corner Blocks
$^1/_4$ yd. deep dark blue print for Cabin Corner Blocks A-1 and B-1
$^1/_4$ yd. dark blue print for Cabin Corner Blocks A-1, A-2, B-1 and B-2
$^1/_4$ yd. dark brown/blue print for Cabin Corner Blocks A-1, B-1, A-4 and B-4
$^1/_4$ yd. dark blue floral print for Cabin Corner Blocks A-2 and B-2
$^1/_4$ yd. dark green fabric for Cabin Corner Blocks A-2, B-2, A-4 and B-4
$^1/_4$ yd. light tan/burgundy print for Cabin Corner Blocks A-3 and B-3
$^1/_4$ yd. dark blue fabric for Cabin Corner Blocks A-4 and B-4

Directions

All seam allowances are $^1/_4$" wide.

Fan Blocks

1. Sew each Template A to the curved edge of a Template B (Diagram 1). Make a total of 41 fans.

2. Appliqué a fan to the center of the wrong side of each of the dark-blue paisley $5^3/_4$" squares.

   Appliqué a fan to the right side in the center of each of the $5^3/_4$" squares of tan paisley, tan/green floral print, brown/black print, and the blue/green prints. You should have a total of 41 fan squares (Diagram 2). Set aside.

Diagram 1   **Diagram 2**

Cabin Corner Blocks A-1, A-2, A-3, and A-4

Refer to the quilt photo and to Diagram 17 on page 34.

1. To make Cabin Corner Block A-1, cut $1^1/_4$"-wide strips from the cream, cream/red pindot, and cream/blue pindot fabrics, cutting across the fabric width, selvage to selvage. Cut additional strips as you need them to complete the 2 blocks required.

2. Cut $1^1/_4$"-wide strips from the deep dark blue print, dark blue print and dark brown/blue print fabrics

in a similar manner. For easier handling, you may cut the strips into 2 equal lengths, approximately 20" to 22" long.

3. Cut 1 square each, $1^1/_4$" x $1^1/_4$", from a cream and a pindot strip. Position the cream square in the upper left corner of one of the muslin squares. Pin. Place the pindot square on top of it, right sides together and raw edges even. Stitch $^1/_4$" from the lower edge. Press the pindot square toward the muslin square (Diagram 3).

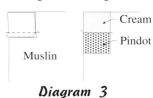

Diagram 3

4. Place a dark strip from step 2 on top of the 2 squares with right sides together and raw edges even with the bottom and inner edge of the squares. Stitch $^1/_4$" from the long raw edge. Press the strip toward the muslin and trim even with the top edge of the muslin square (Diagram 4).

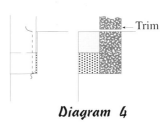

Diagram 4

5. Place a pindot fabric strip on top of the strips with raw edges even with the bottom and inner edges and stitch $^1/_4$" from the bottom raw edge. Press the strip toward the muslin and trim even with the outer edge of the muslin square (Diagram 5).

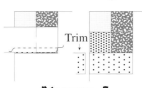

Diagram 5

6. Continue adding strips in alternating fashion, using the light strips on the left side of the block and the dark strips on the right (Diagram 6). Make 2 Cabin Corner Block A-1s in this manner. Set aside.

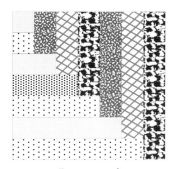

Diagram 6

7. Repeat steps 1 through 6 above to make 6 Cabin Corner Block A-2s, using the dark blue print, dark blue floral print, and the dark green fabrics on the right side of the block (Diagram 7).

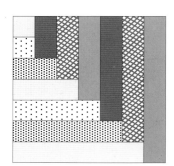

Diagram 7

8. Repeat steps 1 through 6 above to make 8 Cabin Corner Block A-3s, using the tan/green floral print, tan/red floral print, and tan/burgundy print fabrics on the right side of the block (Diagram 8).

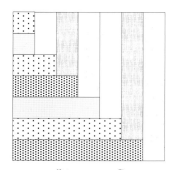

Diagram 8

9. Repeat steps 1 through 6 above to make 4 Cabin Corner Block A-4s, using the dark green, dark brown/blue print, and dark blue solid fabrics on the right side of the block (Diagram 9).

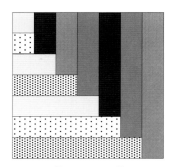

Diagram 9

Cabin Corner Blocks B-1, B-2, B-3, and B-4

1. To make Cabin Corner Block B-1, cut 1¼"-wide strips from the cream, cream/red pindot, cream/blue pindot, deep dark blue print, dark blue print, and dark brown/blue print fabrics as described in steps 1 and 2 of Cabin Corner Block As above.

2. Cut 1 square each, 1¼" x 1¼", from a cream and a pindot strip. Position the cream square in the upper left corner of one of the muslin squares. Pin. Place the pindot square on top of it, right sides together and raw edges even. Stitch ¼" from the inner right edge. Press the square toward the muslin square (Diagram 10).

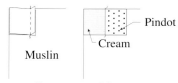

Diagram 10

3. Place a dark strip on top of the cream squares with right sides together and raw edges even with the bottom and inner edge of the squares. Stitch ¼" from the long raw edge. Press the strip toward the muslin and trim even with the left edge of the muslin square (Diagram 11).

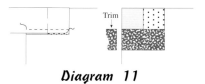

Diagram 11

4. Place a pindot fabric strip on top of the strips with raw edges even with the bottom and inner edges and stitch ¼" from the inner raw edge. Press the strip toward the muslin and trim even with the outer edge of the muslin square (Diagram 12).

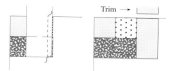
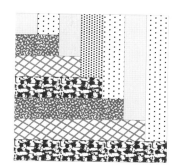

Diagram 12

5. Continue adding strips in alternating fashion, placing the dark strips on the left side of the block and the light strips on the right (Diagram 13). Make 4 Cabin Corner Block B-1s. Set aside.

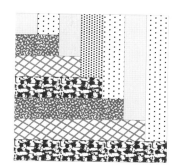

Diagram 13

6. Repeat steps 1 through 5 to make 8 Cabin Corner Block B-2s, using the dark-blue print, dark-blue floral print, and the dark-green fabrics on the left side of the block (Diagram 14).

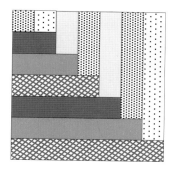

Diagram 14

7. Repeat steps 1 through 5 to make 6 Cabin Corner Block B-3s, using the tan/green floral print, tan/red floral print, and tan/burgundy print fabrics on the left side of the block (Diagram 15).

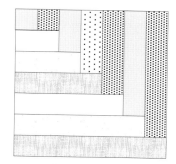

Diagram 15

8. Repeat steps 1 through 5 to make 2 Cabin Corner Block B-4s, using the dark-green, dark-brown/blue print, and dark-blue fabrics on the left side of the block (Diagram 16).

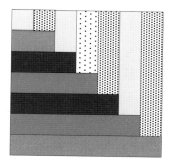

Diagram 16

Quilt Top Assembly

1. Referring to the quilt photo and to Diagram 17 on page 34, arrange the Cabin Corner and Fan blocks in 9 rows of 9 blocks each. Each Cabin Corner Block label, i.e., "A-1," refers to a diagonal row.

2. Sew the blocks together in rows, then sew the rows together, being careful to match seam lines between the blocks.

3. Sew the dark green inner border strips together to make one long piece. Measure the quilt top for borders with mitered corners following the directions on page 93. (It should measure 47¾" square.) Cut 4 border strips, each at least 53" long and sew to the quilt top, mitering the corners.

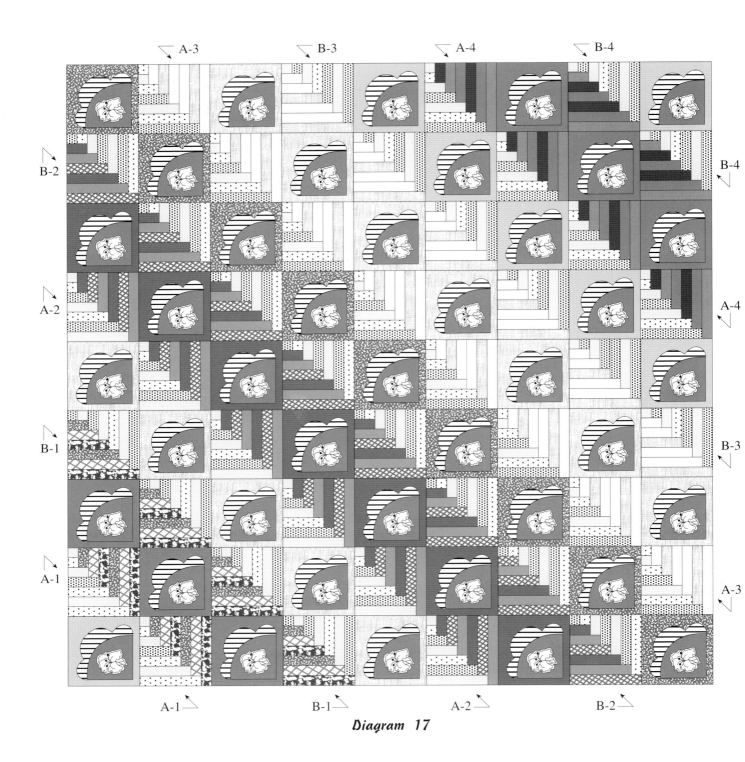

Diagram 17

4. Sew 2 of the brown print outer border strips together to make one long strip. Repeat with 2 additional strips. Cut the remaining strip in half and add a half-strip to each of the longer strips. From each long strip, cut 2 outer border strips, each 51¼" long.

Sew a brown print outer border strip to the left and to the right side of the quilt top.

Sew a 7" square of tan/red floral print to opposite ends of the remaining two outer border strips. Sew to the top and bottom edges of the quilt top.

Finishing

Refer to pages 94-96 in the "General Directions."

1. Mark the quilting lines on the quilt top in the top outer border (Diagram 18). Rotate the diagram 90° for each remaining side. Mark diagonal quilting lines through each tan/red floral corner square. Mark additional quilting lines as desired.

2. Sew the blue/tan backing strips together with the widest one between the two narrower ones as shown on page 94. Use ¼"-wide seams and press the seams open. Trim the resulting piece to 68" square.

3. Layer the quilt top with batting and backing; baste.

4. Quilt by hand or machine with white thread.

5. Bind the edges with blue/tan print double-layer bias binding.

Brown print outer border

Dark green inner border

Diagram 18

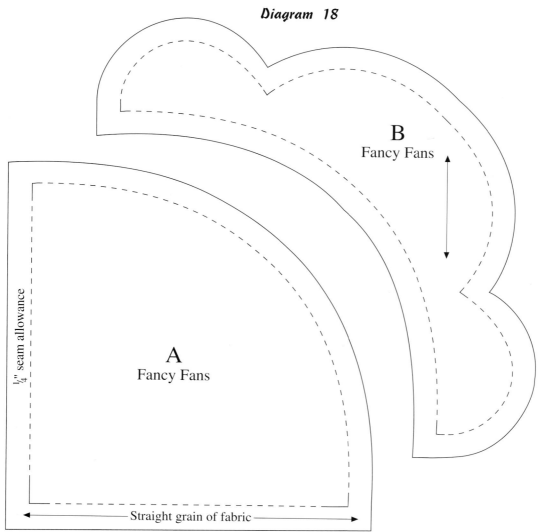

B
Fancy Fans

A
Fancy Fans

¼" seam allowance

Straight grain of fabric

35

Zippy Zebra

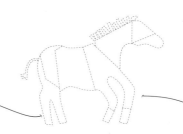

Finished Size: 28½" x 40½"

Materials (44"-wide fabric)	**Cutting** (Use templates on pages 43-47.)
Note: With the exception of the blue background print and the black-and-white polka dot fabric for the zebra, all fabrics in this quilt are solid-colored. You may substitute subtle prints if desired.	
½ yd. black for zebra	7 strips, each 1" x 12" 8 strips, each 1" x 27" 1 Template P (tail) 10 strips, each ¾" wide and varying from 1" to 2" long, for mane
¼ yd. white for zebra	7 strips, each 1" x 12" 6 strips, each 1" x 27"
⅛ yd. black-and-white polka dot for zebra	3 strips, each 1" x 12" 3 strips, each 1" x 27"
⅛ yd. bright yellow for zebra	2 strips, each 1" x 27"
¼ yd. rose for zebra and striped triangle blocks	3 strips, each 1" x 12", for zebra stripes See additional cutting information in directions for "Striped Triangle Blocks" on page 40.
1 yd. blue print for background	1 piece, 25¼" x 28½" 1 piece, 7½" x 14½" 2 strips, each 2¼" x 5½" 8 Template D 2 Template E
¼ yd. light yellow for moon	1 Template Q (moon)
¼ yd. pink	1 strip, 1" x 22" See additional cutting information in directions for "Striped Triangle Blocks" on page 40.
⅛ yd. yellow-orange	1 strip, 1" x 22"
⅛ yd. each of 5 graduated shades of orange for diamond blocks	1 strip, 1" x 22", from each of the 5 colors

(continued on page 38)

Materials *(continued)*	***Cutting*** *(continued)*
³/₄ yd. salmon for triangles	4 Template A 8 Template C
¹/₄ yd. pale green for lower corners	2 Template E
1¹/₄ yds. blue-green	1 piece, 32" x 43
¹/₂ yd. blue/black print for binding	4¹/₄ yds. of 2"-wide bias strips
32" x 44" piece of batting White thread for quilting	

Directions

All seam allowances are ¹/₄" wide.

Section 1—Zebra

1. Sew the 1" x 12" strips of black, white, polka dot and rose fabrics together along the long edges to make a string-pieced unit, alternating the colors as desired and aligning grain-line arrows with seams. Press seams toward the darker color. Cut 1 each of Templates I, L, M, and N (Diagram 1).

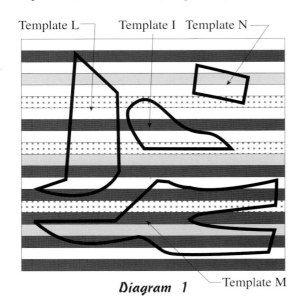

Diagram 1

2. Sew the 1" x 27" strips of black, white, polka dot, and yellow fabrics together along the long edges to make a string-pieced unit, alternating the colors as desired. Press seams toward the darker color. Cut 1 each of Templates F, G, H, J, K and O, aligning the grain line arrow on each with a seam line in the string-pieced unit.

3. Sew Piece G to Piece H (Diagram 2). Sew pieces N and O to Piece J (Diagram 3).

4. Sew Template I to the zebra face. Sew Template K to the chest (Diagram 4). Sew Template L to the midsection, stitching in the direction of the arrows. Then sew Template M to zebra, stitching in direction of arrows (Diagram 5).

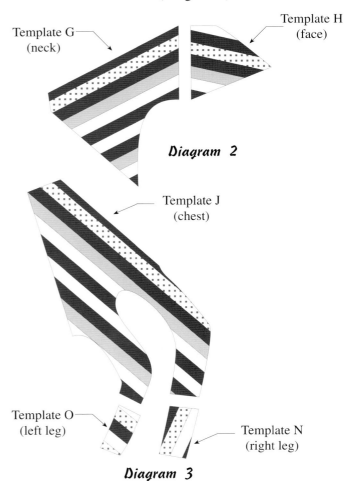

Diagram 2

Diagram 3

5. Prepare the zebra for appliqué by turning under ¼" on all raw edges. Baste. (See "Appliqué." on page 91.)

6. Referring to the quilt photo and Diagram 12 on page 41, position the zebra on the 25¼" x 28½" blue print background fabric. Center it with the hooves 1⅜" above the bottom raw edge. Use a few pins to hold it in place.

7. Prepare the tail (Template P) for appliqué by turning under ¼" on all raw edges, except short edge at top of tail. Position the tail on the background fabric and pin in place, tucking the short end under the zebra body.

8. Repeat step 7 with the ear (Template F), positioning it above the zebra head, and tucking the straight edge under the zebra body.

9. Repeat step 7 with the 1½"-wide pieces for the mane, positioning them as desired along top of zebra neck and tucking one short end of each under the zebra body.

10. Remove the zebra and appliqué the tail, ear and mane in place on the background fabric. Replace the zebra and appliqué in place. Appliqué the moon to background fabric, turning under the ¼"-wide seam allowance. Set Section 1 aside.

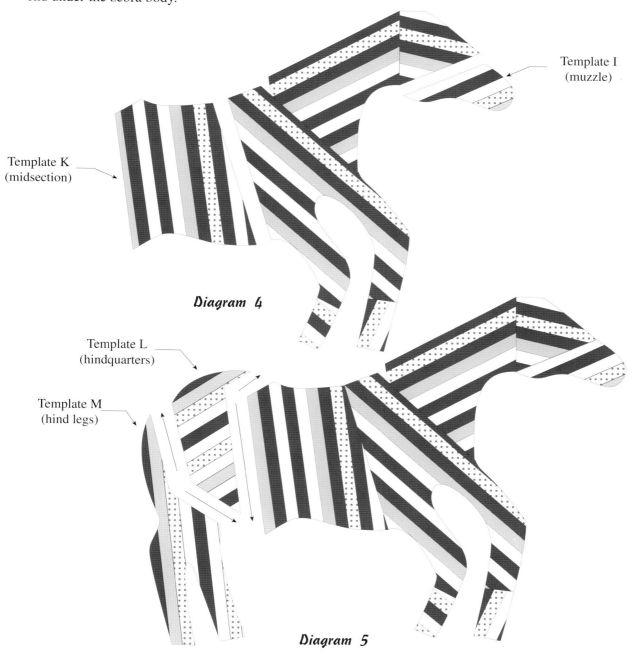

Template I (muzzle)

Template K (midsection)

Diagram 4

Template L (hindquarters)

Template M (hind legs)

Diagram 5

Section 2—Striped Diamonds

1. Arrange the 1" x 22" strips of fabric (pink, yellow-orange and 5 shades of orange) in order from dark to light. Sew together to make a finished string-pieced unit measuring 4" x 22". Cut 5 Template B, aligning the grain line arrow with a seam line in the unit.

2. Arrange the salmon-colored pieces A and C with the striped diamonds in diagonal rows. Sew together in rows. Sew the rows together, adding a Piece A to the upper left and lower right corners last (Diagram 6).

3. To complete Section 2, add a 2¼" x 5½" strip of blue print fabric to each end and press the seams toward the strips (Diagram 7). Set Section 2 aside.

Section 3—Striped Triangle Blocks

1. From the remaining rose and pink fabrics, cut 4 strips, each 34" long and varying in width from ¾" to 1", for a total of 8 strips. Sew the strips together along the long edges, alternating the colors as desired. Press seams toward the darker color. The resulting strip-pieced unit should measure at least 5" x 34".

2. Cut 4 Template D, aligning the grain line arrow with a seam line in the string-pieced unit. Turn the template over and cut 4 Template D reversed so that you have 2 sets of triangles that are mirror images of each other (Diagram 8).

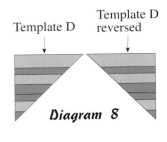

Diagram 8

3. Sew each striped triangle to a blue print triangle (Template D). Arrange the completed striped triangle blocks as shown in Diagram 9. Sew blocks together. The resulting strip should measure 4" x 28½". Set aside Section 3.

Section 4

1. Sew each blue print Template E to a pale green Template E along the long edges. Press seam allowance toward darker fabric in each square (Diagram 10).

Diagram 10

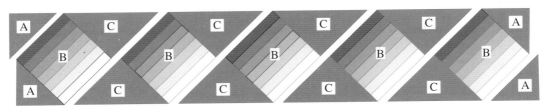

Diagram 6

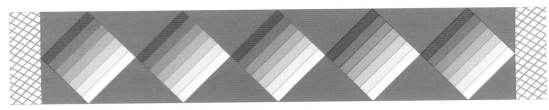

Diagram 7

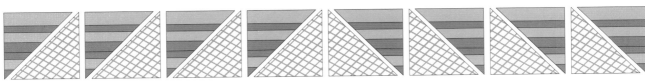

Diagram 9

40

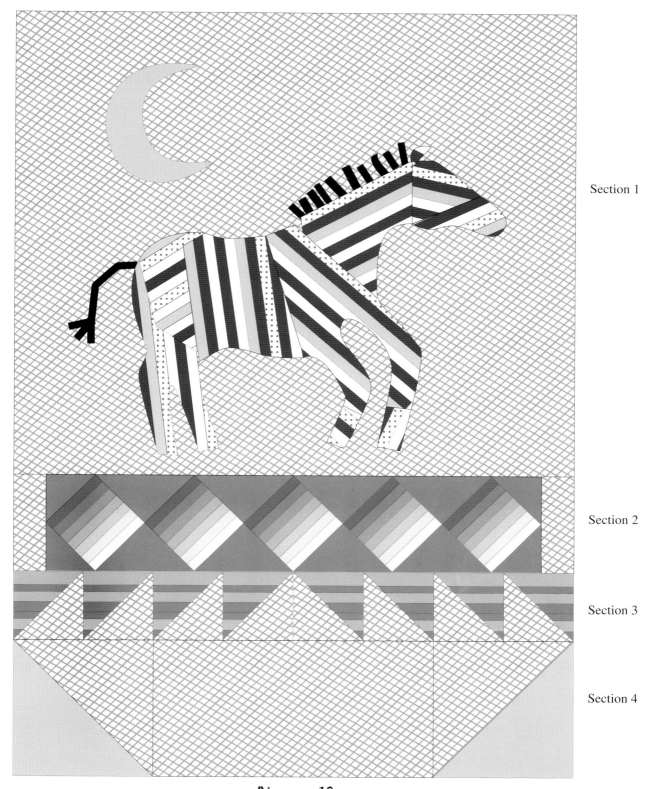

Section 1

Section 2

Section 3

Section 4

Diagram 12

41

2. Sew 1 Piece E/E to each short end of the
   7¹/₂" x 14¹/₂" blue print piece (Diagram 11).

Diagram 11

Quilt Top Assembly

Refer to Diagram 12 on page 41.

1. Sew Section 1 to the top edge of Section 2.
2. Sew Section 3 to Unit 1/2. Sew Section 4
   to Unit 1/2/3.

Finishing

Refer to pages 94-96 in the
"General Directions."

1. Mark one quilting line
   around zebra, following
   zebra's contours. Repeat for
   moon. Mark remaining
   quilting lines on the quilt
   top, referring to Diagram 13.

2. Layer the quilt top with
   batting and backing; baste.

3. Quilt by hand or machine,
   using white thread.

4. Bind the edges with double-
   layer bias strips cut from the
   blue/black print bias
   binding.

Diagram 13

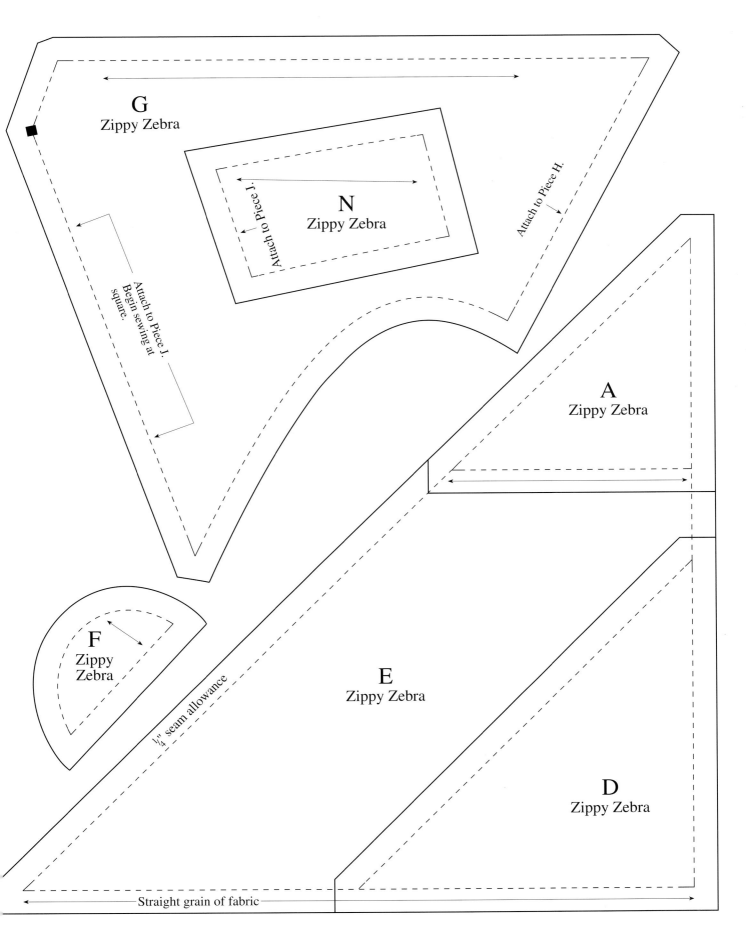

G
Zippy Zebra

N
Zippy Zebra

Attach to Piece J.

Attach to Piece H.

Attach to Piece J.
Begin sewing at
square.

A
Zippy Zebra

F
Zippy
Zebra

E
Zippy Zebra

D
Zippy Zebra

¼" seam allowance

Straight grain of fabric

43

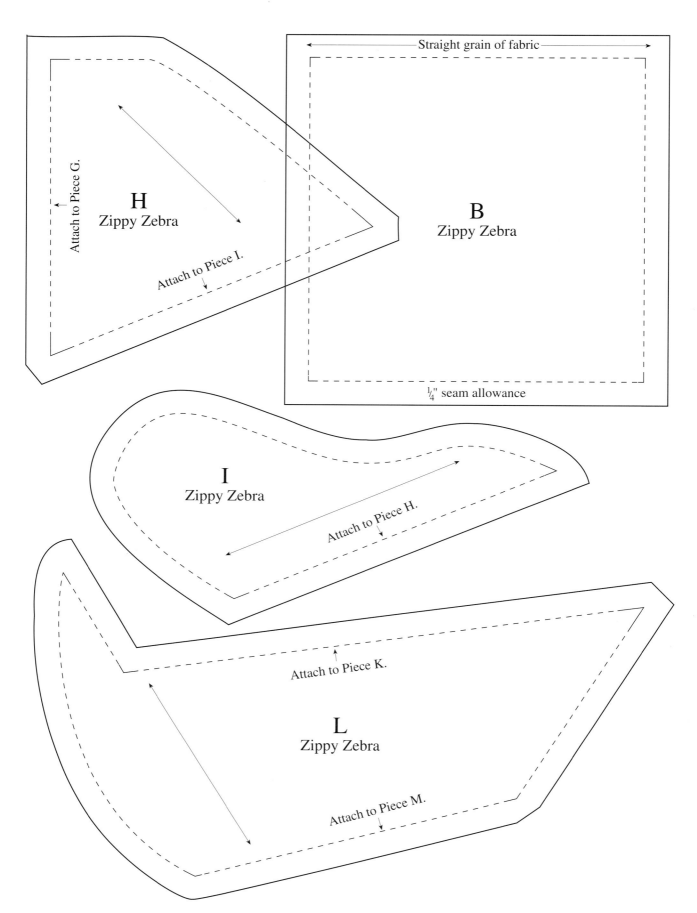

H
Zippy Zebra

Attach to Piece G.

Attach to Piece I.

Straight grain of fabric

B
Zippy Zebra

$\frac{1}{4}$" seam allowance

I
Zippy Zebra

Attach to Piece H.

Attach to Piece K.

L
Zippy Zebra

Attach to Piece M.

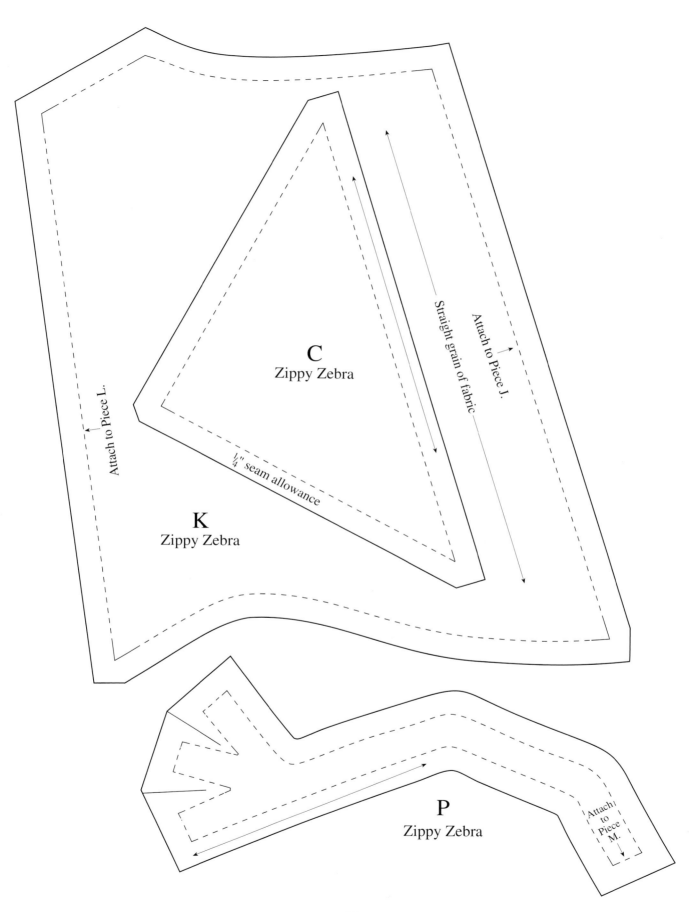

C
Zippy Zebra

K
Zippy Zebra

P
Zippy Zebra

Attach to Piece L.

Attach to Piece J.

Straight grain of fabric

¼" seam allowance

Attach to Piece M.

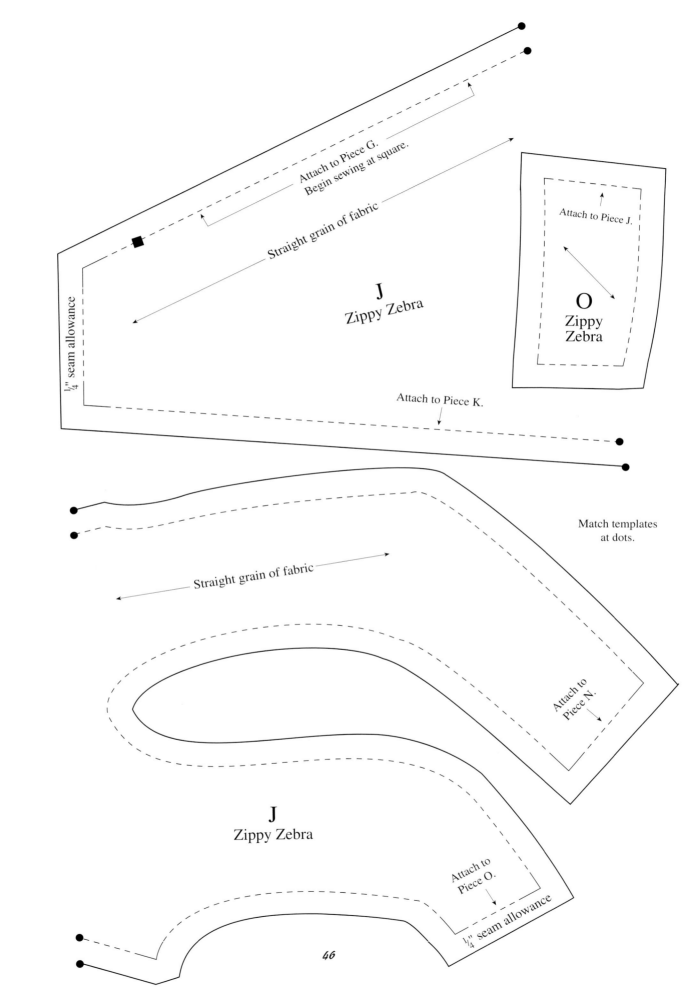

Attach to Piece G.
Begin sewing at square.

Straight grain of fabric

Attach to Piece J.

J
Zippy Zebra

O
Zippy
Zebra

¼" seam allowance

Attach to Piece K.

Match templates
at dots.

Straight grain of fabric

Attach to
Piece N.

J
Zippy Zebra

Attach to
Piece O.

¼" seam allowance

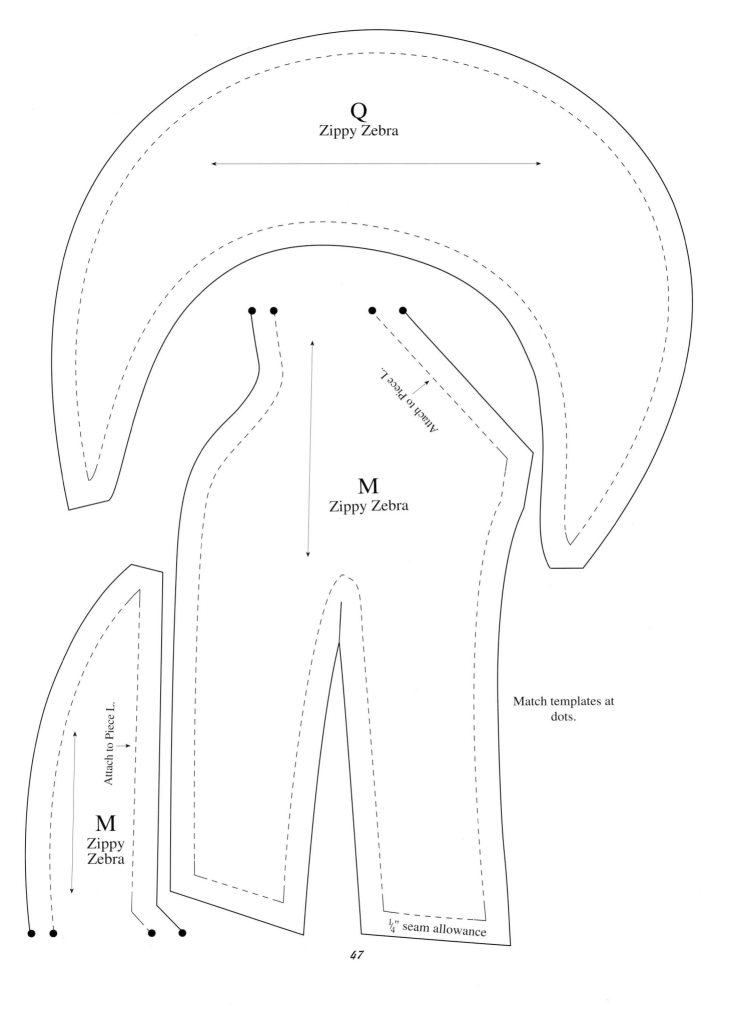

Q
Zippy Zebra

M
Zippy Zebra

Attach to Piece L.

Attach to Piece L.

M
Zippy
Zebra

Match templates at
dots.

$\frac{1}{4}$" seam allowance

All-American Kids

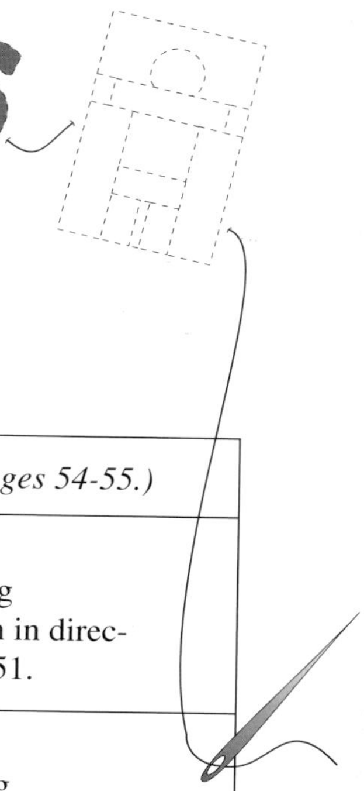

Finished Size: 31½" x 31½"
Finished Flag Size: 8" x 12"
Finished Kids Block Size: 4" x 6"

Materials (44"-wide fabric)	**Cutting** (Use templates on pages 54-55.)
½ yd. red-and-white pindot for skirts and flag	3 strips, each 1" x 6½", for flag 4 strips, each 1⅛" x 11½", for flag See additional cutting information in directions for "Girl Block A" on page 51.
¼ yd. white solid-colored fabric for skirts, dresses, flag, flag ends, and boy blocks	3 strips, each 1" x 6½", for flag 4 strips, each 1⅛" x 11½", for flag 2 strips, each 1" x 8½", for flag ends 5 pieces, each 2¼" x 4½", for upper background in boy blocks 10 pieces, each 1⅝" x 4", for side background in boy blocks 5 pieces, each ¾" x 1¾", for background between pant legs See additional cutting information in directions for girl blocks on pages 51-52.
Scrap of dark blue print for flag background	1 piece, 3½" x 5½"
¼ yd. dark red fabric for shirts and dresses	2 pieces, each 1¼" x 3½", for shirt sleeves 2 pieces, each 2" x 2¼", for shirts See additional cutting information in directions for flag and dresses on page 50 and "Girl Block B" on page 52.
⅛ yd. medium blue solid for shirts	3 pieces, each 1¼" x 3½", for shirt sleeves 3 pieces, each 2" x 2¼", for shirts
⅛ yd. dark blue solid for pants	5 pieces, each 1¼" x 2¼", for upper pants 10 pieces, each 1¼" x 1¾", for pant legs
⅛ yd. each of light yellow, tan, and brown for faces and hands	See cutting information in directions for girl and boy blocks on pages 50-52.
Scrap of green-and-white checked fabric	2 pieces, each 1¼" x 3½", for dress sleeves

(continued on page 50)

Materials *(continued)*	***Cutting*** *(continued)*
$^7/_8$ yd. pink for girl blocks and binding	5 pieces, each $2^1/_4$" x $4^1/_2$", for upper background in girl blocks 5 Template C and 5 of C reversed 10 pieces, each $1^3/_4$" x $1^3/_4$", for leg background 5 pieces, each $^3/_4$" x $1^3/_4$", for background between legs $3^1/_4$ yds. total of 2"-wide bias strips
$^1/_8$ yd. slate blue fabric for dress sleeves	3 Template E and 3 of E reversed
$^1/_2$ yd. sea-green solid-colored fabric for outer corner blocks	4 Template F
$^1/_4$ yd. pale green solid-colored fabric for outer corner blocks	4 Template G
$^1/_2$ yd. blue print for mitered borders	4 strips, each 4" x 34"
1 yd. light blue fabric for backing	1 piece, 34" x 34"
34" x 34" piece of batting White thread for quilting Dark brown, light green and red embroidery floss 20 small white buttons for stars on flag	

Directions

All seam allowances are $^1/_4$" wide.

Flag

1. Assemble the upper striped flag section, using the 1" x $6^1/_2$" strips of white and red-and-white pindot fabric. Begin with a red strip and end with a white strip. Press seams toward the red strips. The finished piece should measure $3^1/_2$" x $6^1/_2$". Assemble the lower striped flag section in the same manner, using the $1^1/_8$" x $11^1/_2$" strips. The finished piece should measure $5^1/_2$" x $11^1/_2$". (See Diagram 1.)

2. Assemble the flag unit as shown, sewing the $3^1/_2$" x $5^1/_2$" dark blue rectangle to the left end of the smaller striped section. Add the larger striped section, then sew the 1" x $8^1/_2$" strips to the flag ends (Diagram 1).

Diagram 1

Boy Blocks

Following the piecing directions below, make 2 boy blocks with red shirts and dark blue pants and 3 boy blocks with medium blue shirts and dark blue pants.

1. Sew a $^3/_4$" x $1^3/_4$" white strip between each pair of $1^1/_4$" x $1^3/_4$" dark blue pant legs. Press seams toward the legs. Add a dark blue $1^1/_4$" x $2^1/_4$" upper pant piece to the top edge of the legs, then add the 2" x $2^1/_4$" shirt (either red or medium blue) as shown in Diagram 2. Press the seams toward the upper pant piece.

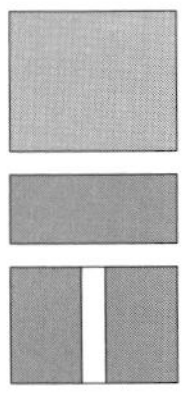

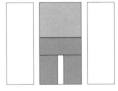

Diagram 2

2. Sew a $1^5/_8$" x 4" white strip to each long edge of the shirt/pants unit (Diagram 3). Press seams toward the pants.

Diagram 3

3. For each block, cut 2 hands, each 1" x $1^1/_4$", and a head (Template A), using your choice of light yellow, tan or brown fabrics. Sew 1 hand to each short end

of each red or blue 1¼" x 3½" sleeve piece (Diagram 4). Press seams toward the sleeves.

Diagram 4

4. Prepare each head for appliqué by turning under and basting the seam allowance along the outer curved edge only. Do not turn under bottom edge of head. (See "Appliqué" on page 91.) Fold in half and finger crease the fold to mark the center of the head. Do the same with the sleeve/hand unit. Pin the prepared head to the sleeve with centers matching and stitch ⅛" from the raw edges (Diagram 5). Do not press.

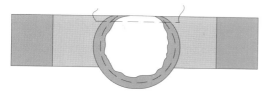

Diagram 5

5. Sew a 2¼" x 4½" white background piece to the top edge of the sleeve/hand unit, catching the head in the stitching. Press the seam toward the sleeves. Appliqué the head to the background (Diagram 6).

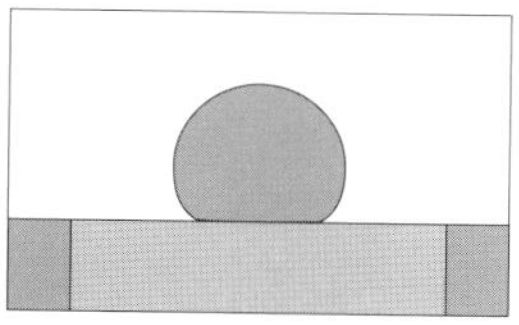

Diagram 6

6. Sew the sleeve/hand/head unit to the top edge of the shirt/pants unit (Diagram 7).

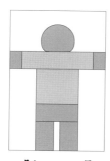

Diagram 7

Girl Block A (checked sleeves and striped skirt)

Make 2 blocks following the block piecing directions below.

1. From the red pindot fabric and from the white solid, cut 4 strips, each 9½" long and varying in width from 1" to 1½". Sew the strips together

along the long edges and press the seams toward the red strips. The resulting string-pieced unit should be at least 3½" wide.

2. Cut 2 Template B for skirts, adjusting the template position so that the stripes are positioned differently in each skirt (Diagram 8).

Diagram 8

3. For each block, cut 1 head (Template A), 2 hands, and 2 legs from your choice of light yellow, tan or brown fabric. For legs, cut pieces 1⅛" x 1¾" and for hands, cut pieces 1" x 1¼". Sew 1 hand to each short end of each 1¼" x 3½" sleeve piece as shown in Diagram 4 for the boy blocks. Press seams toward the sleeves.

4. Assemble 2 leg sections as shown in Diagram 9, using 2 legs, two 1¾" pink squares, and a ¾" x 1¾" pink background piece in each one.

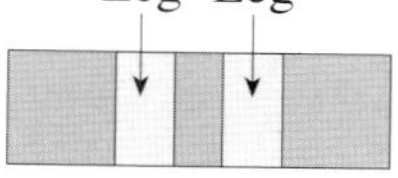

Diagram 9

5. Assemble each skirt section, using the striped skirt made in step 1 and 1 each of the pink Template C and C reversed (Diagram 10).

Diagram 10

6. Sew the leg section to the bottom edge of the skirt section (Diagram 11).

7. Prepare head for appliqué and sew to the sleeve/hand unit as directed for the boy blocks in step 4 (Diagram 5). Add a 2¼" x 4½" pink background piece and appliqué the head as directed in step 5 (Diagram 6).

Diagram 11

8. Sew the head/sleeve unit to the top edge of the skirt unit (Diagram 12). Press the seam toward the sleeves.

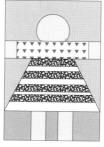

Diagram 12

Girl Block B (blue sleeves, striped skirt)

1. Cut 4 strips from the dark red fabric, each 12" long and varying in width from 1" to 1½". Repeat with the white fabric. Sew the strips together along the long edges and press the seams toward the red strips. The resulting string-pieced unit should be at least 4" wide.

2. Cut 3 Template D for skirts, adjusting the template position so the stripes are positioned differently in each skirt as shown in Diagram 8 for Girl Block A on page 51.

3. Piece the leg section as shown in Diagram 9 for Girl Block A on page 51.

4. Assemble the sleeve/hand/background sections and sew to the skirt (Diagram 13).

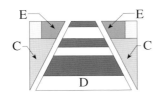

Diagram 13

5. For each of the 3 blocks, cut a head, hands and legs from your choice of light yellow, tan or brown fabrics as described in step 3 for Girl Block A on page 51.

6. Prepare the head for appliqué as shown in Diagram 5 on page 51. Sew it to the top edge of the dress section as you did for Girl Block A. Do not press.

7. Sew a 2¼" x 4½" pink background piece to the top edge of the dress section, catching the head in the stitching. Press the seam toward the dress. Appliqué in place.

8. Sew the head/dress unit to the top edge of the leg section to complete the block (Diagram 14).

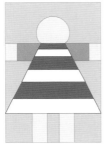

Diagram 14

Quilt Top Assembly

1. Make 4 corner blocks by sewing each Template F to a Template G (Diagram 15).

Diagram 15

2. Referring to Diagram 17 on page 53, arrange the completed kids, corner blocks, and flag in horizontal rows. Sew the blocks together in rows, then sew the rows together to complete the quilt top.

3. Sew the blue borders to the quilt, mitering the corners. (See "Adding Borders" on page 92.)

Finishing

Refer to pages 94-96 in the "General Directions."

1. Embroider hair on the girl and boy blocks, using dark brown embroidery floss. Satin stitch bow ties on the boy blocks, using red embroidery floss on the blue shirts and green embroidery floss on the red shirts (Diagram 16).

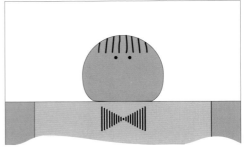

Diagram 16

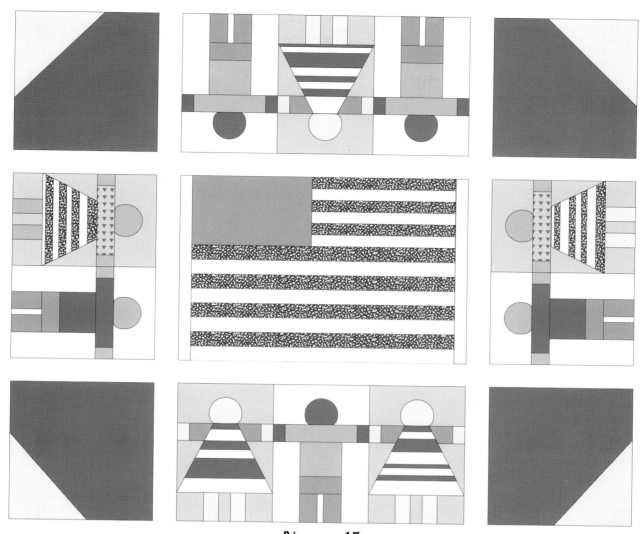

Diagram 17

2. Using red embroidery floss and an outline stitch, embroider a meandering line through the center of the white strips at the sides and bottom edges of the flag block (Diagram 18).

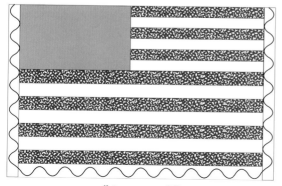

Diagram 18

3. Mark quilting designs around each boy and girl block as desired. Mark quilting lines through each flag stripe. Mark quilting lines in the borders and corner blocks as shown in Diagram 19 on page 54.

4. Layer the quilt top with batting and backing; baste.

5. Quilt by hand or machine, using white thread.

6. Sewing through all layers, attach buttons to blue rectangle in flag (4 rows of 5 buttons each).

7. Bind the edges with double-layer pink bias binding.

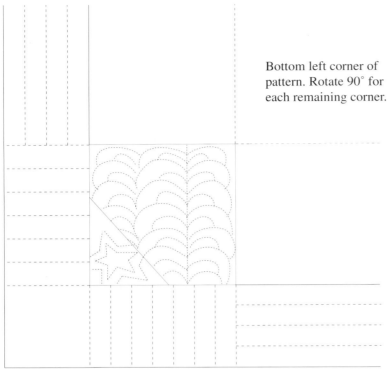

Bottom left corner of pattern. Rotate 90° for each remaining corner.

Diagram 19

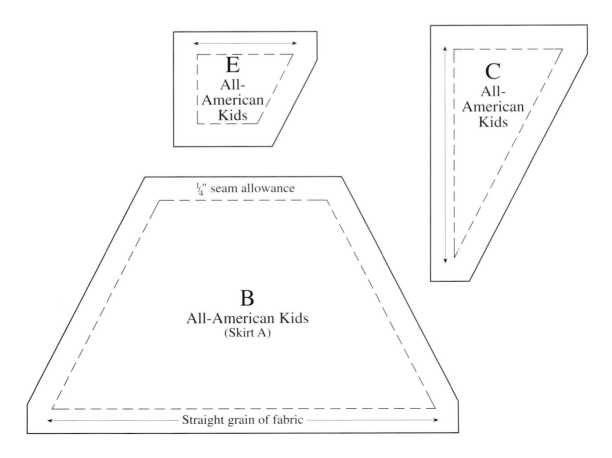

E
All-
American
Kids

C
All-
American
Kids

¼" seam allowance

B
All-American Kids
(Skirt A)

Straight grain of fabric

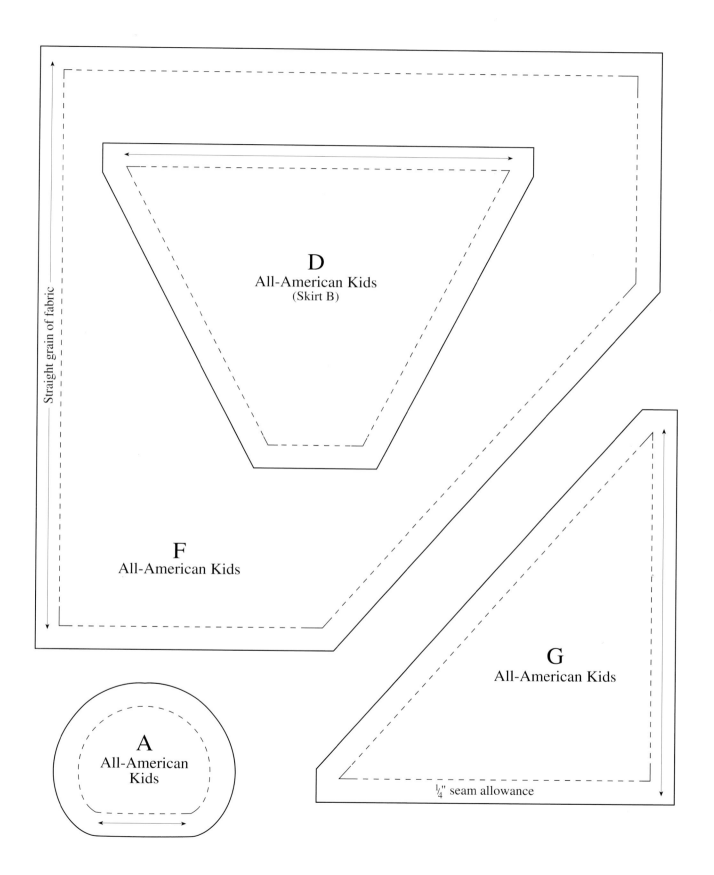

D
All-American Kids
(Skirt B)

Straight grain of fabric

F
All-American Kids

G
All-American Kids

A
All-American
Kids

¼" seam allowance

Sailing, Sailing

Finished Size: 27 x 32$^1/_4$"
Finished Block Size: 4$^1/_2$" x 6$^1/_4$"

Materials *(44"-wide fabric)*	**Cutting** *(Use templates on page 61.)*
$^1/_8$ yd. light blue fabric for block corners and sky	See cutting information in directions for "Sailboat Blocks" on page 58.
$^1/_4$ yd. medium blue fabric for blocks	9 pieces, each 1$^1/_2$" x 4" See additional cutting information in directions for "Sailboat Blocks."
$^1/_4$ yd. light purple fabric for block background and water	9 Template C and 9 Template C reversed See additional cutting information in directions for "Sailboat Blocks."
Scraps of red (10" x 14"), yellow (10" x 10"), and green (6" x 6") for sails	See cutting information in directions for "Sailboat Blocks."
$^1/_4$ yd. white fabric for sails	See cutting information in directions for "Sailboat Blocks."
$^1/_8$ yd. black/blue print for masts and sails	9 pieces, each $^3/_4$" x 5" See additional cutting information in directions for "Sailboat Blocks."
$^1/_4$ yd. brown fabric for boat hulls	9 Template B
$^1/_4$ yd. tan fabric for lattice strips	6 pieces, each 1$^1/_4$" x 6$^3/_4$" 4 pieces, each 1$^1/_4$" x 15$^1/_2$" 2 pieces, each 1$^1/_4$" x 22$^1/_4$"
2 yds. slate blue fabric for borders, backing and binding	1 piece, 31" x 36"* 1 strip, 5$^1/_2$" x 17" 2 strips, each 5$^1/_2$" x 27$^1/_2$" 1 strip, 5$^1/_2$" x 27" 3$^1/_2$ yds. of 2"-wide bias strips
31" x 36" piece of batting White thread for quilting	
*Cut the large piece for the backing first and set aside.	

Directions

All seam allowances are $1/4$" wide.

Sailboat Blocks

1. From the light blue fabric, cut 1 strip, $1^7/8$" x 38". From the medium blue fabric, cut 1 strip, $2^5/8$" x 38". Sew together on long edges. Press seam toward darker fabric. Cut 9 Template A from string-pieced unit for block backgrounds (Diagram 1.) Set aside.

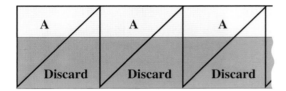

Diagram 1

2. From light blue fabric, cut 1 strip, $1^7/8$" x 16". From light purple fabric, cut 1 strip, $3^5/8$" x 16". Sew strips together and press the seam toward the darker fabric. Cut 9 pieces, each $1^1/2$" x 5", for background (Diagram 2). Set aside.

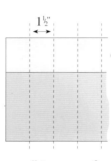

Diagram 2

3. From red fabric, cut 4 strips, each 13" long, in widths varying from $3/4$" to $1^1/4$". Repeat with white fabric. Sew strips together in alternating colors and widths to make a piece at least $4^1/2$" wide. Press seams toward red strips. Cut 3 Template A for sails, varying the template location so sails are all different (Diagram 3). Set aside.

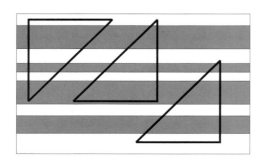

Diagram 3

4. Repeat step 3 with the black/blue print and yellow fabrics, cutting strips 9" long and varying the widths as before. Cut 2 of Template A from each unit. Repeat with 5"-long strips of green and white fabrics. Cut 1 of Template A (Diagram 4). Set aside.

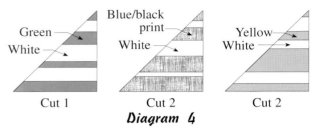

Diagram 4

5. Stitch each sail to a medium-blue/light blue background triangle (Template A). Add a $1^1/2$" x 4" strip of medium-blue background to the bottom edge (Diagram 5).

Diagram 5

6. Fold each $3/4$" x 5" black/blue mast strip in half lengthwise with wrong sides together and pin one to the right-hand edge of each sail. Stitch (Diagram 6).

Place a light blue/light purple background unit on top of the mast, right sides together, and stitch on top of previous stitching. Press the seam toward the background unit so the folded mast lies on top of the sail (Diagram 7).

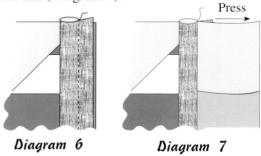

Diagram 6   **Diagram 7**

7. Sew 1 Template C and 1 Template C reversed to the bottom edge of each brown boat hull, Template B (Diagram 8).

Diagram 8

8. Sew a hull to the bottom of each sail unit (Diagram 9).

9. Referring to the quilt photo for color placement, lay out the sails in 3 rows. Sew blocks together in horizontal rows, adding 6³/₄"-long tan lattice strips between the blocks as shown in Diagram 10.

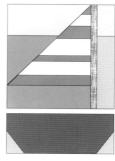

Diagram 9

Quilt Top Assembly

1. Join the block rows, adding the 15¹/₂" tan sashing strips at the top and bottom and between the rows and making sure that the vertical sashing strips are aligned with each other.

2. Add a 22¹/₄"-long tan sashing strip to each side of the quilt top.

3. Sew the 17"-long slate blue border strip to the top edge of the quilt, then add a 27¹/₂"-long border to each side, and finally, add the 27"-long border to the bottom edge.

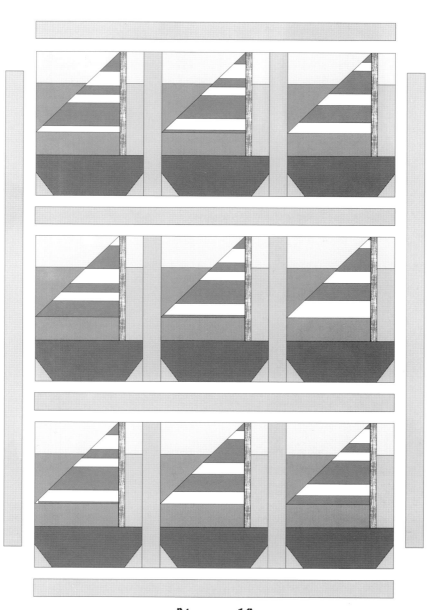

Diagram 10

Finishing

Refer to pages 94-96 in the "General Directions."

1. Mark quilting lines on the quilt top, using Template 1 on page 61 and referring to Diagram 11.

2. Layer the quilt top with batting and backing; baste.

3. Quilt by hand or machine, using white thread.

4. Bind the edges with double-layer slate blue bias binding.

Diagram 11

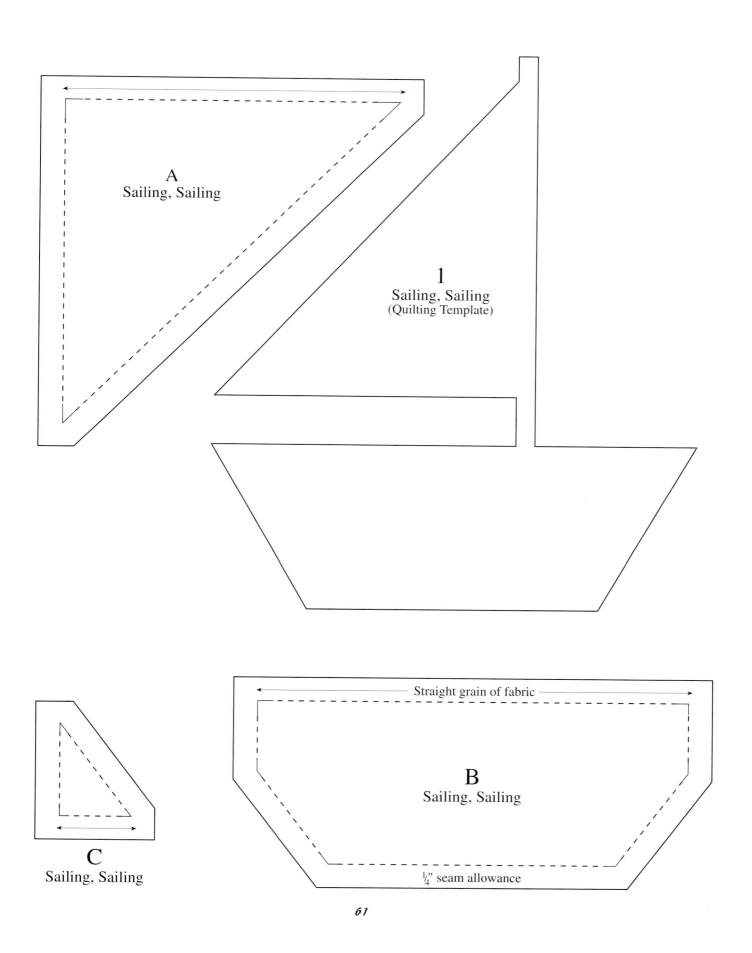

A
Sailing, Sailing

1
Sailing, Sailing
(Quilting Template)

C
Sailing, Sailing

Straight grain of fabric

B
Sailing, Sailing

$\frac{1}{4}$" seam allowance

Pine View Cabin

Finished Size: 15$\frac{1}{2}$" x 35$\frac{1}{4}$"

This quilt plan has been divided into sections and each piece is numbered by section. (See Assembly Diagrams 1 and 2.) You can rotary cut most pieces; templates are provided for some and are also labeled section by section. To make it easy to assemble this quilt, lay out the pieces for each section on a flat surface as you cut them, or place them in position on a large piece of batting tacked to the wall. If neither is possible, label each piece with the appropriate section and number to avoid confusion later.

Materials (44"-wide fabric)	*Cutting* (Use templates on pages 66-68.)
$\frac{7}{8}$ yd. green/orange print for background	1 piece, 3$\frac{3}{4}$" x 15$\frac{1}{2}$", for Piece A 2 pieces, each 1$\frac{3}{4}$" x 5$\frac{1}{2}$", for Piece B-1 1 piece, 1$\frac{3}{4}$" x 2$\frac{1}{2}$", for Piece B-3 2 pieces, each 2" x 5$\frac{3}{4}$", for Piece C-1 1 piece, 2" x 3", for Piece C-3 2 pieces, each 3$\frac{1}{2}$" x 3$\frac{3}{4}$", for Piece D-1 1 Template D-2 and 1 Template D-2 reversed 2 pieces, each 1$\frac{1}{2}$" x 3", for Piece E-1 2 pieces, each 3$\frac{5}{8}$" x 8$\frac{1}{4}$", for Piece F-1 1 Template G-1 and 1 Template G-1 reversed 2 Template G-3 1 Template H-1 and 1 Template H-1 reversed 2 Template H-3 2 pieces, each 1$\frac{1}{2}$" x 2$\frac{3}{4}$", for Piece I-1 2 pieces, each 2$\frac{1}{4}$" x 4$\frac{1}{4}$", for Piece J-1 2 pieces, each 2$\frac{1}{4}$" x 3$\frac{3}{8}$", for Piece J-3
$\frac{1}{8}$ yd. tan/rose print for chimney pots and strips in Section K	2 pieces, each 1$\frac{3}{4}$" x 2", for Piece B-2 2 pieces, each 1$\frac{1}{4}$" x 3$\frac{1}{2}$", for Piece K-1 2 pieces, each 1$\frac{7}{8}$" x 3$\frac{1}{2}$", for Piece K-4 1 piece, 1$\frac{1}{4}$" x 3$\frac{1}{2}$", for Piece K-6
$\frac{1}{4}$ yd. red print for chimneys, walls and tree trunks	2 pieces, each 1$\frac{1}{2}$" x 2", for Piece C-2 2 pieces, each 1" x 2$\frac{1}{4}$", for Piece J-2 1 piece, 1$\frac{1}{4}$" x 2$\frac{1}{4}$", for Piece J-4 See additional cutting information in directions for "Cabin Walls" on page 65.
$\frac{1}{8}$ yd. red/white floral print for walls	See additional cutting information in directions for "Cabin Walls" on page 65.
$\frac{1}{8}$ yd. dark green print for roof	2 Template D-3 2 Template D-4 1 piece, 1$\frac{1}{2}$" x 10$\frac{1}{2}$", for Piece E-2

(continued on page 64)

Materials (continued)	**Cutting** (continued)
Scrap of green/yellow floral print for house gable	1 Template D-5
1/4 yd. dark green solid for trees, checkerboard sections, and window	2 squares, each 1 1/4" x 1 1/4", for Piece D-6 3 Template G-2 3 Template H-2 1 strip, 1 1/2" x 11", for Piece I-2 3 strips, each 1" x 9", for pieces K-3 and K-5
1/8 yd. dark red solid for checkerboard and window	2 squares, each 1 1/4" x 1 1/4", for Piece D-6 3 strips, each 1" x 9", for pieces K-3 and K-5
1/8 yd. green fabric for wall posts	2 pieces, each 1 5/8" x 6 1/2", for Piece F-2 2 pieces, each 1 1/2" x 2 1/2", for Piece F-3
Scrap of purple fabric for door	1 piece, 2" x 4", for Piece F-6
1/8 yd. green/black print for door posts and lintel	2 pieces, each 1" x 4", for Piece F-4 1 piece, 1" x 3", for Piece F-5
1/8 yd. green/black print fabric for diamonds in lawn	5 squares, each 1 3/4" x 1 3/4", for Piece F-9
1/8 yd. light green fabric for the lawn	4 Template F-10 8 Template F-11
1 yd. gray/multicolor floral for backing and strips	1 piece, 18 1/2" x 38 1/2", for backing 1 strip, 1 1/4" x 15 1/2", for Piece F-12 2 squares, each 3 1/2" x 3 1/2", for Piece K-2 1 strip, 5 1/2" x 15 1/2", for Piece L
1/8 yd. blue/yellow floral print for strip beneath trees	1 strip, 1 3/4" x 15 1/2", for Piece J-5
1/8 yd. pale green print for strip for Section K	1 piece, 2 1/2" x 15 1/2", for Piece K-7
1/4 yd. light blue fabric for binding	3 yds. of 1 1/4"-wide bias strips
18 1/2" x 38 1/2" piece of batting 3 buttons, each 1/2" in diameter Dark green thread for quilting	

Directions

All seam allowances are 1/4" wide.

Cabin—Sections A through E

1. Referring to Assembly Diagram 1 on page 69, assemble Section B and Section C. Sew sections A, B, and C together, making sure the chimneys, Piece C-2, are positioned under the chimney pots, Piece C-3. Set aside.

2. To assemble Section D, sew Pieces D-2 and D-4 together. Add D-1 to the left-hand side of D-2/D-4. Add D-3 to the right-hand side. Sew to the left-hand side of Piece D-5. Assemble the remainder of the section in the same manner, and sew to the right-hand side of Piece D-5 (Diagram 1 on page 65).

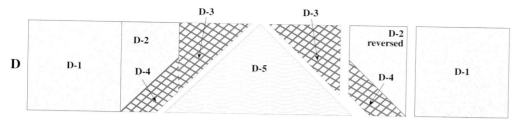

Diagram 1

3. Using the dark green and dark red 1¼" squares, make checkerboard D-6 (Diagram 2). Appliqué to the gable, Piece D-5 (Diagram 3). See "Appliqué" on page 91.

Diagram 2

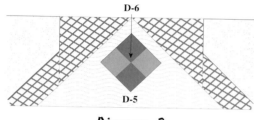

Diagram 3

4. Assemble Section E and sew to the bottom edge of Section D. Sew sections D/E and sections A/B/C together, making sure the gable, Piece D-5, is centered under the background, Piece C-3.

Cabin Walls and Door—Section F

1. Cut 8 strips, each 7½" long, from the red print and 8 strips, each 7½" long from the red/white floral. Cut them in widths varying from ¾" to 1¼".

2. Alternating colors and widths, sew the strips together to make a piece that measures 6" x 7½". From the string-pieced unit, cut 1 piece 2½" x 7", for Piece F-7, and 2 pieces, each 2½" x 3½", for Piece F-8 (Diagram 4).

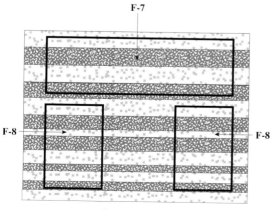

Diagram 4

3. Sew the door posts, F-4, to the long sides of the door, F-6. Add the lintel, F-5, to the top edge (Diagram 5).

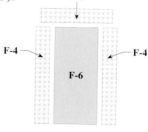

Diagram 5

4. Sew a Piece F-3 to the bottom edge of each cabin wall, Piece F-8. Sew F-3/F-8 to each side of the door. Add Piece F-7 to the top edge of door and walls, then add a wall post, F-2, to each side (Diagram 6).

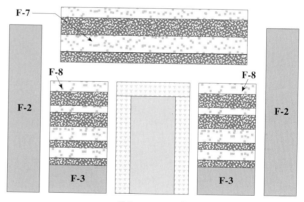

Diagram 6

5. Sew pieces F-9, F-10, and F-11 together in diagonal rows as numbered. Sew the rows together, then add Piece F-10 to the upper left and lower right corners to complete the strip (Diagram 7).

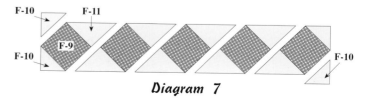

Diagram 7

6. Sew the completed strip to the bottom edge of the cabin. Add a background Piece F-1 to each side of the completed cabin, then add Piece F-12 to the bottom edge. See Assembly Diagram 1 on page 69. This completes Section 1.

Pine Trees—Sections G through J

Assemble Sections G, H, I, and J, referring to Assembly Diagram 2 on page 70.

1. Pin Section G to Section H, carefully centering each Piece H-2 under a Piece G-2. Stitch.

2. Pin Section J to Section I, carefully centering the tree trunks, Pieces J-2 and J-4, under the trees. Stitch.

3. Pin Section G/H to Section I/J, carefully matching the seams at the outer edges of the trees. Stitch. Set aside.

Sections K through L

Assemble Sections K and L, referring to Assembly Diagram 2 on page 70.

1. To make the checkerboard, Pieces K-3 and K-5, sew the dark red and dark green 1" x 9" strips together, alternating the colors. Press all seams in one direction.

2. Cut 8 pieces, each 1" x 3$\frac{1}{2}$", from the resulting unit. Set 2 strips aside for Piece K-3. For each Piece K-5, sew 3 strips together, checkerboard style (Diagram 8).

Piece K-5

Diagram 8

3. Assemble Section K, referring to Assembly Diagram 1. Sew Piece K-7 to the bottom edge, then add Piece L.

4. Sew Section G/H/I/J to the top edge of Section K/L. This completes Section 2.

5. Sew Section 1 to Section 2 to complete the quilt top assembly.

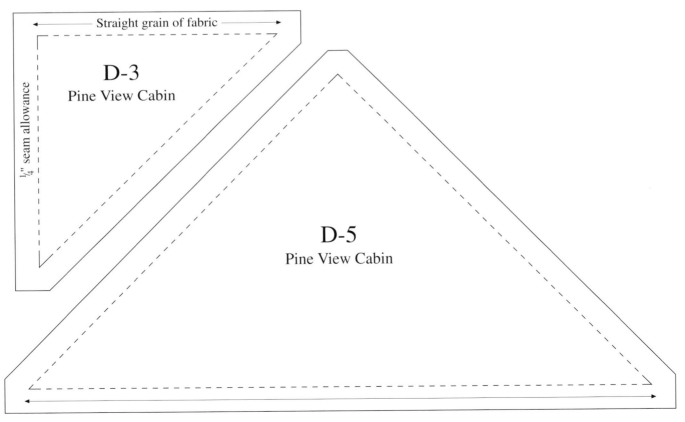

Straight grain of fabric

$\frac{1}{4}$" seam allowance

D-3
Pine View Cabin

D-5
Pine View Cabin

Finishing

Refer to pages 94-96 in the "General Directions."

1. Mark quilting lines on the quilt top (Diagram 9).

2. Layer the quilt top with batting and backing; baste.

3. Quilt by hand or machine, using dark green thread.

4. Bind the edges with single-layer, light blue bias binding.

5. Sew the three buttons to the quilt top, referring to the quilt photo for placement.

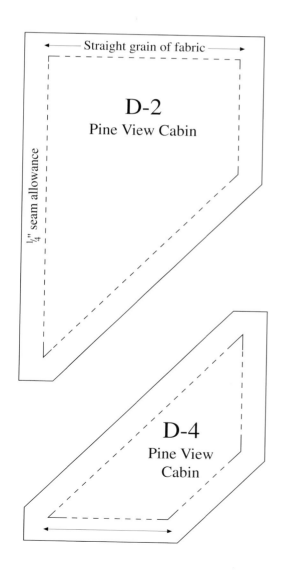

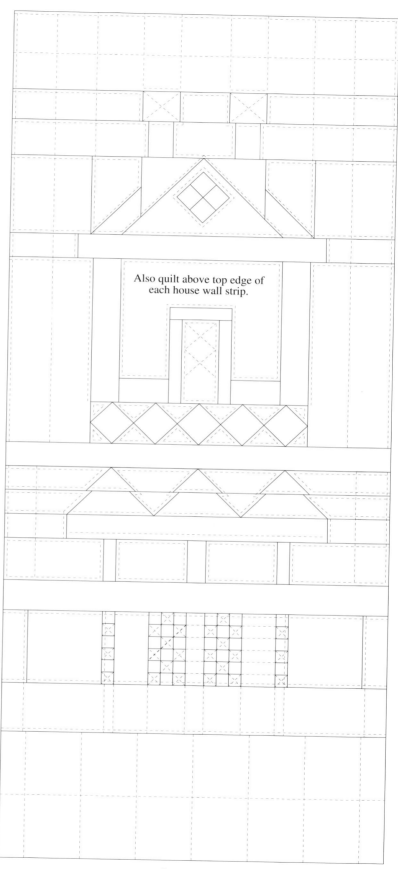

Also quilt above top edge of each house wall strip.

Diagram 9

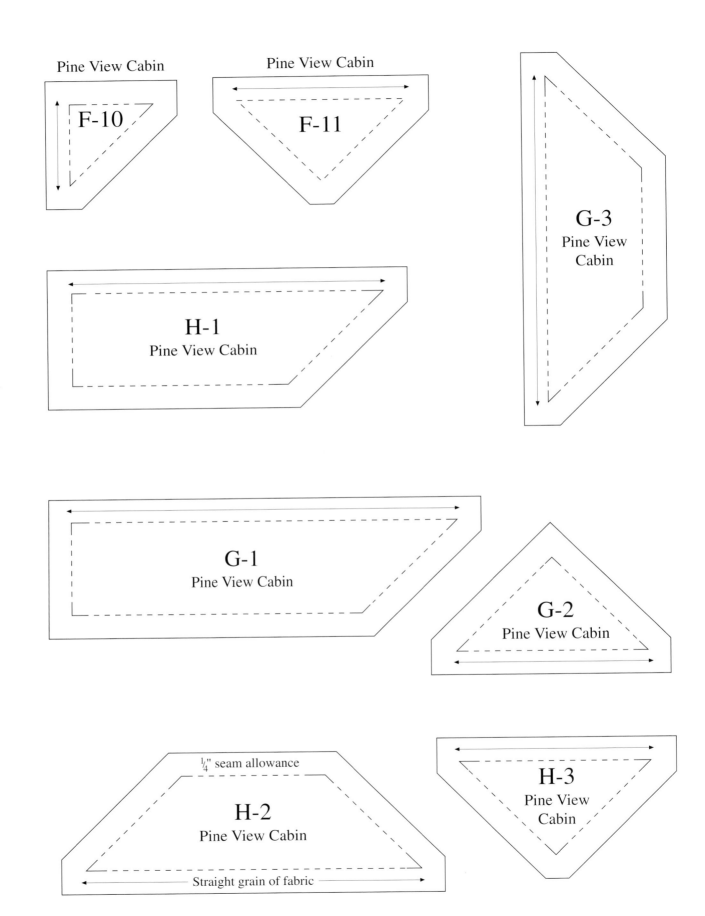

Pine View Cabin

F-10

Pine View Cabin

F-11

G-3
Pine View
Cabin

H-1
Pine View Cabin

G-1
Pine View Cabin

G-2
Pine View Cabin

¼" seam allowance

H-2
Pine View Cabin

Straight grain of fabric

H-3
Pine View
Cabin

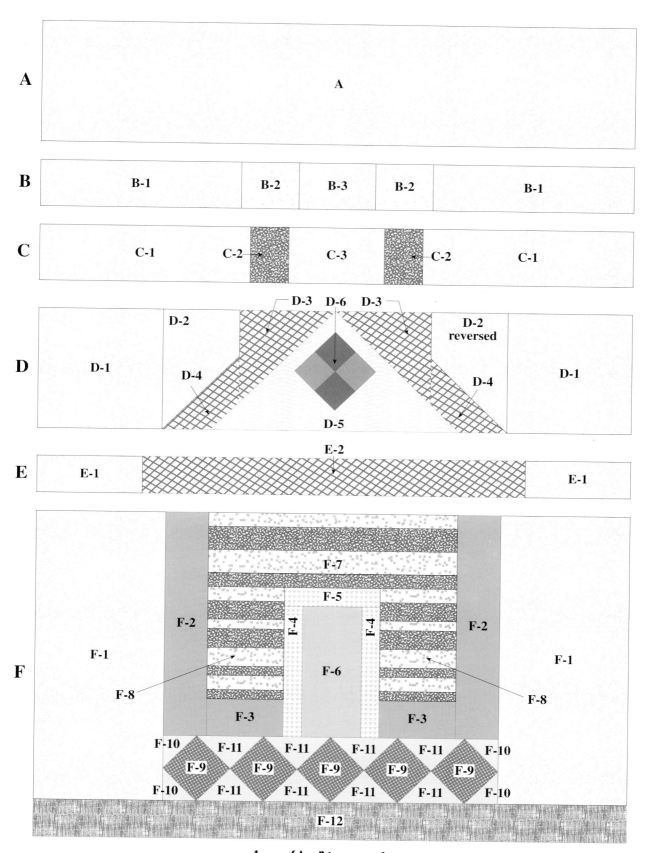

Assembly Diagram 1

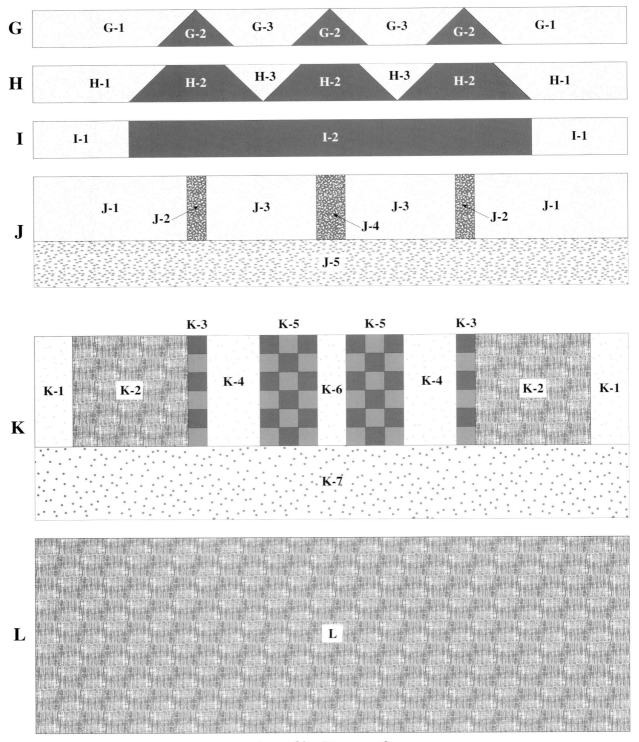

Assembly Diagram 2

American Home

Finished Size: 62$\frac{1}{2}$" x 62$\frac{1}{2}$" (at widest point), 57" x 57" (at narrowest point)
Finished Bordered Ninepatch Block Size: 7$\frac{1}{2}$" x 7$\frac{1}{2}$"
Finished House Block Size: 11" x 11"

Materials *(44"-wide fabric)*	**Cutting** *(Use templates on pages 79-81.)*
$\frac{1}{4}$ yd. maroon print #1 for Ninepatch blocks	4 strips, each 2" x 32"
$\frac{1}{4}$ yd. light blue print for Ninepatch blocks	5 strips, each 2" x 32"
2$\frac{1}{4}$ yds. green-and-white checked gingham with small overprinted pattern for Ninepatch block borders and inner border	16 pieces, each 2" x 6$\frac{1}{2}$" See additional cutting information in directions for "Inner Borders" on page 75.
$\frac{1}{4}$ yd. gray-green dot print for Ninepatch block borders	16 pieces, each 2" x 6$\frac{1}{2}$" See additional cutting information in directions for "Inner Borders" on page 75.
$\frac{1}{4}$ yd. beige print #1 for Ninepatch block borders	16 pieces, each 2" x 6$\frac{1}{2}$"
$\frac{1}{4}$ yd. beige print #2 for Ninepatch block borders	16 pieces, each 2" x 6$\frac{1}{2}$"
$\frac{1}{8}$ yd. blue print for sky in House blocks	8 pieces, each 1$\frac{3}{4}$" x 2$\frac{1}{4}$" 4 pieces, each 1$\frac{3}{4}$" x 2$\frac{1}{2}$" 4 Template B, cut from wrong side of fabric 4 Template C
$\frac{1}{2}$ yd. maroon solid for chimney, house side, inner borders, and appliqués*	8 pieces, each 1$\frac{1}{4}$" x 1$\frac{3}{4}$" (chimneys) 3 squares, each 1$\frac{3}{4}$" x 1$\frac{3}{4}$" (large heart) 4 squares, each 4" x 4" (house sides) 2 squares, each 2" x 2" (small checkerboard) 2 pieces, each 1$\frac{5}{8}$" x 1$\frac{7}{8}$" (large checkerboard) See additional cutting information in directions for "Inner Borders" on page 75.
$\frac{1}{8}$ yd. brown print for rooftop	4 Template A
$\frac{1}{8}$ yd. maroon floral print for house front	4 Template D, cut from wrong side of fabric
Scraps of yellow print for window appliqués*	8 Template 1*
$\frac{1}{8}$ yd. slate blue for appliqués*	4 pieces, each 1$\frac{3}{4}$" x 2$\frac{3}{4}$" (doors) 2 each of Template E and F 3 Template 2* 2 squares, each 2" x 2" (small checkerboard) 2 pieces, each 1$\frac{5}{8}$" x 1$\frac{7}{8}$" (large checkerboard) 1 Template 3*

(continued on page 73)

Materials *(continued)*	**Cutting** *(continued)*
³/₈ yd. light pink-and-green calico for House Block borders	4 strips, each 2¹/₂" x 7¹/₂" (top) 8 strips, each 2¹/₂" x 9¹/₂" (sides) 4 strips, each 2¹/₂" x 11¹/₂" (bottom)
¹/₄ yd. pale green for inner border	See cutting information in directions for "Inner Borders" on page 75.
¹/₈ yd. light slate blue for stars	6 Template 4*
¹/₈ yd. of brown print for flowers	3 Template 5*
¹/₈ yd. of light maroon for hands	2 Template 6 and 2 Template 6 reversed*
¹/₄ yd. medium brown for outer border ¹/₄ yd. gray for outer border ¹/₄ yd. maroon print #2 for outer border ¹/₄ yd. maroon print #3 for outer border ³/₄ yd. maroon/gray print for outer border	See cutting information in directions for "String-Pieced Outer Borders" on page 76.
³/₄ yd. off-white for binding	8¹/₂ yds. of 1¹/₄"-wide bias
4 yds. off-white fabric for backing	2 pieces, each 2 yds. long
70" x 70" piece of batting	
*See directions for cutting and preparing appliqués on pages 91-92.	

Directions

All seam allowances are ¹/₄" wide.

Ninepatch Blocks

1. Sew a 2" x 32" strip of maroon print #1 to each long edge of a 2" x 32" light blue print strip. Press the seams toward the maroon print. Using a rotary cutter, ruler, and mat, cut 16 segments, each 2" wide from resulting unit (Diagram 1).

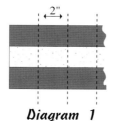

Diagram 1

2. Repeat, sewing a light blue print strip to each long edge of each of the 2 remaining maroon print #1 strips. Cut each unit into 16 segments, each 2" wide, for a total of 32 (Diagram 2).

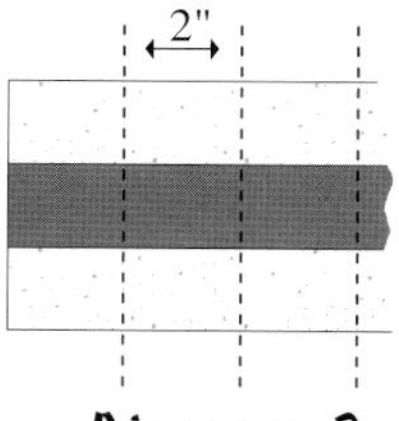

Diagram 2

3. Arrange the segments into 16 Ninepatch blocks as shown in Diagram 3. Sew the segments together to complete each Ninepatch unit.

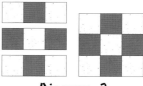

Diagram 3

4. Add the 2" x 6¹/₂" border strips in numerical order, pressing all seams toward the borders. Sew a strip of green gingham to the top edge of each Ninepatch unit, ending the stitching 1" from the right-hand side of the block. Sew a strip of beige #2 to left-hand edge of the block, then sew a strip of beige #1 to the bottom. Sew dot-print strip to the right-hand side (Diagram 4).

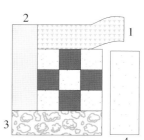

Diagram 4

5. Complete the seam at the top right corner of the block.

6. Lay out the completed Ninepatch blocks in 4 rows of 4 blocks each, making sure that the top borders are all green gingham. Sew the blocks together in rows. Sew the rows together to complete the center of the quilt (Diagram 5). For complete block layout, see Diagram 17 on page 77.

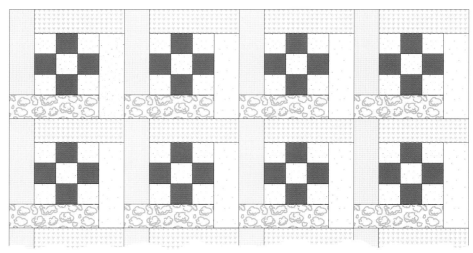

Diagram 5
(Rows 1 and 2 of 4)

House Blocks

Make each of the 4 House blocks in the following manner:

1. Assemble the sky/chimney strip by sewing 2 blue sky (1³/₄" x 2¹/₄"), 1 blue sky (1³/₄" x 2¹/₂") and 2 maroon chimney pieces together, placing the 2¹/₂" sky strip between the 2 chimneys. Sew the sky (Template B) to the upper left edge of the house front (Template D), making sure to use the wrong side of each fabric as the right side. Add the brown roof (Template A) to the blue sky (Template C). Sew a 4" maroon square to the bottom edge of the roof (Diagram 6).

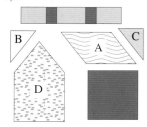

Diagram 6

2. Sew the house front section to the side section, stitching in the direction of the arrows (Diagram 7).

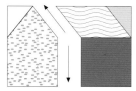

Diagram 7

3. Sew the sky/chimney unit to the top edge of the house. Appliqué 2 yellow print hearts (Template 1) to the side of the house. (See "Appliqué" on page 91.) Appliqué the 1³/₄" x 2³/₄" slate door to the house front, being careful to center it under the peak of the roof (Diagram 8).

Diagram 8

4. Sew a 2¹/₂" x 7¹/₂" calico border strip to the top of each house. Sew a 2¹/₂" x 9¹/₂" strip to each side of the house. Sew a 2¹/₂" x 11¹/₂" strip to the bottom of each house (Diagram 9). Set the completed blocks aside.

Diagram 9

Inner Borders

The directions that follow are general directions for creating 4 different, randomly pieced inner borders. This is your chance to design your own borders or to create ones that are similar to those on the quilt shown in the photo on page 71.

1. For each border, cut a strip of freezer paper, 11" x 30". Following Diagram 10 as a guide, divide each strip into several sections, including some triangular shapes and one that is approximately 4" wide, but not a true rectangle. In Diagram 10, each of these sections is indicated by an asterisk. Use a pencil and a ruler to draw the shapes on the un-coated side of each strip of freezer paper. Divide each 4"-wide section into several traingular shapes, referring to the quilt photo for ideas.

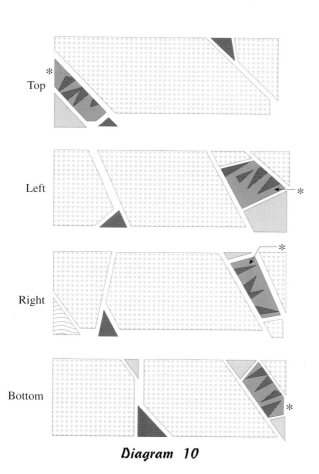

Diagram 10

2. Label each piece in each border strip with a number and a color. Use the green-and-white checked gingham for the larger pieces of the border. Use maroon and pale green for the pieces in the 4"-wide sections (Diagram 11).

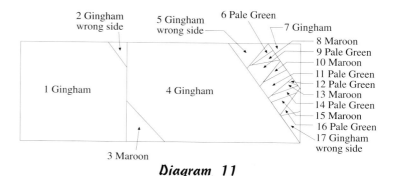

Diagram 11

3. Draw hash marks across each line for matching purposes (Diagram 12). The bottom border is shown in the diagram as an example.

Diagram 12

4. *Working with one border strip at a time*, carefully cut out each shape on the lines. Position each freezer-paper piece, coated side down, on the right side of the desired fabric, leaving at least ¹/₂" allowance between neighboring pieces.

You may want to cut some of the pieces from the wrong side of the gingham for a subtle difference in color. If so, position those pieces on the wrong side of the gingham.

Press with a dry iron so pattern shape adheres to the fabric. Using a sharp pencil and a ruler, draw cutting lines ¹/₄" beyond each edge of each piece (Diagram 13).

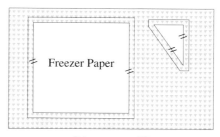

Freezer Paper

Diagram 13

Cut out the pieces on the drawn lines. (You may measure and cut in one step, if you prefer, using a rotary ruler, cutter, and mat.) Extend the hash marks into the seam allowances with light pencil marks as shown in Diagram 13 on page 75.

5. Arrange the cut border pieces in their original positions. Plan the stitching order so that you will always be stitching straight edges together. For example, you will want to sew the maroon and pale green pieces together to complete the 4"-wide section, then sew that section to its neighboring pieces in the border strip.

6. After deciding the stitching order, peel away the freezer paper on the first 2 pieces and pin together, matching hash marks. Stitch and press the seam in one direction. Continue in this manner until the border is completely assembled. Repeat this process to make the remaining 3 border strips.

Border Appliqués

1. Make 1 checkerboard appliqué by sewing the 2" x 2" maroon and blue squares together as shown in Diagram 14.

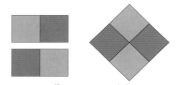

Diagram 14

2. Make the remaining checkerboard appliqué by sewing the $1^5/8$" x $1^7/8$" maroon and blue rectangles together as shown in Diagram 15. Sew the slate blue Template E to the short edges of the checkerboard, then sew the slate blue Template F to the long sides of the checkerboard (Diagram 16).

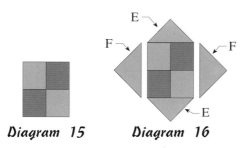

Diagram 15   **Diagram 16**

3. Appliqué the $1^3/4$" maroon squares to the slate blue heart (Template 3), referring to the template for placement. Trim squares even with outer edge of heart.

4. Prepare all appliqués as described on page 91.

5. Position appliqués on the pieced inner borders, referring to the quilt photograph and Diagram 17 on page 77 for placement. Sew in place.

Quilt Top Assembly

1. Sew completed inner borders to the top and bottom edges of the quilt top center. Press the seams toward the borders.

2. Sew a House block to each end of each of the remaining inner border strips, referring to Diagram 17 on page 77 for the correct placement of the blocks. Sew the resulting border strips to the quilt top. Press the seams toward the borders.

String-Pieced Outer Borders

1. Cut 26"-long strips in widths ranging from 1" to 2" from the outer border fabrics (medium brown, gray, maroon print #2, maroon print #3, and maroon/gray print).

2. Arrange the strips in random fashion to make 2 sets of strips. Sew each set together to make a total of 2 units, each 26" x 28".

3. Trace Template G onto 1 of the string-pieced units 4 times as shown in Diagram 18.

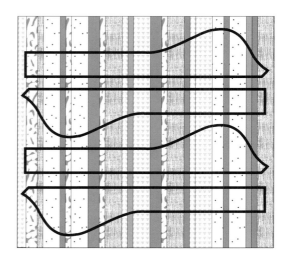

Diagram 18

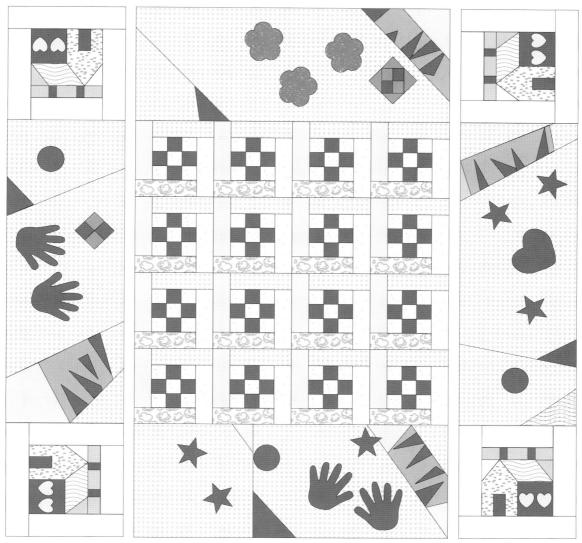

Diagram 17

4. *Reverse the template* and trace 4 times onto the remaining string-pieced unit. Cut out. On the wrong side of each piece, mark the seam intersection at the scalloped end as shown in Diagram 19.

Sew the scalloped border pieces together in pairs (Diagram 20).

Diagram 19

5. Pin a border to each side of the quilt top, placing the marked seam intersections at the seam intersections of the quilt top. Stitch, beginning and ending at the seam intersections (Diagram 21).

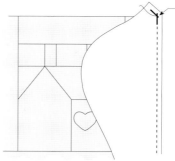

Intersection lines drawn in step 4. Begin and end stitching at this intersection.

Diagram 20

Diagram 21

6. Miter each border corner (Diagram 22).

Finishing

Refer to pages 94-96 in the "General Directions."

1. Mark the quilting lines on the quilt top, referring to diagrams 23, 24 and 25 and the photo. Mark parallel quilting lines on outer borders along each seam and within each fabric.

2. Cut one of the 2-yard pieces of backing in half lengthwise, then sew one piece to each long side of the remaining 2-yard length of backing. Press the seams open and trim the resulting piece to 70" x 70".

3. Layer the quilt top with batting and backing; baste.

4. Quilt by hand or machine. Trim away excess batting and backing even with the shaped edges of the quilt top.

5. Bind the edges with single-layer off-white bias binding.

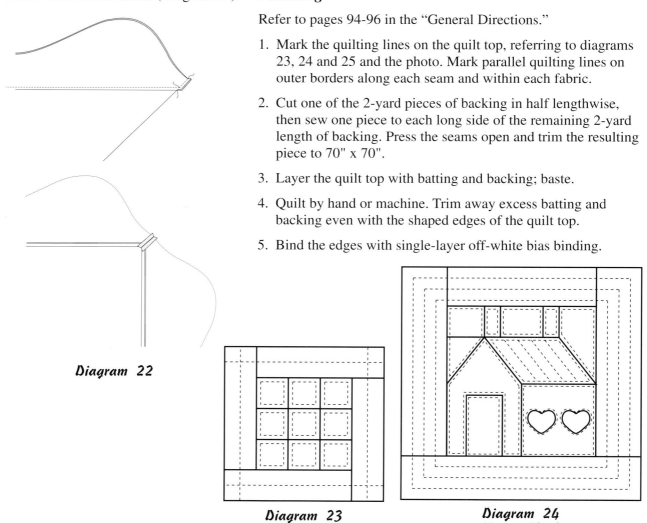

Diagram 22

Diagram 23
Ninepatch Block

Diagram 24
House Block

Quilting lines are randomly drawn in scallop shapes, and around and through appliqués. Refer to photo for ideas.

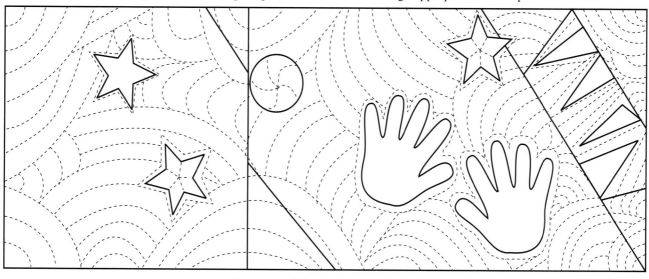

Diagram 25 — Inner Border

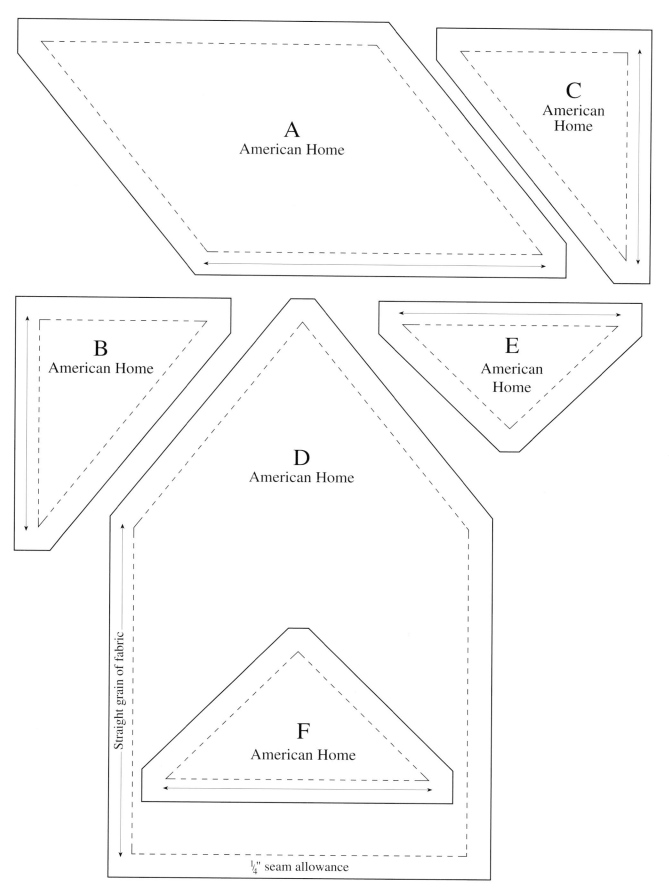

A
American Home

C
American
Home

B
American Home

E
American
Home

D
American Home

Straight grain of fabric

F
American Home

¼" seam allowance

79

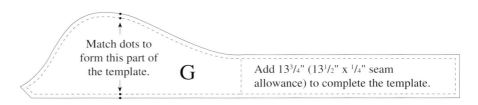

Match dots to form this part of the template.

G

Add 13³/₄" (13¹/₂" x ¹/₄" seam allowance) to complete the template.

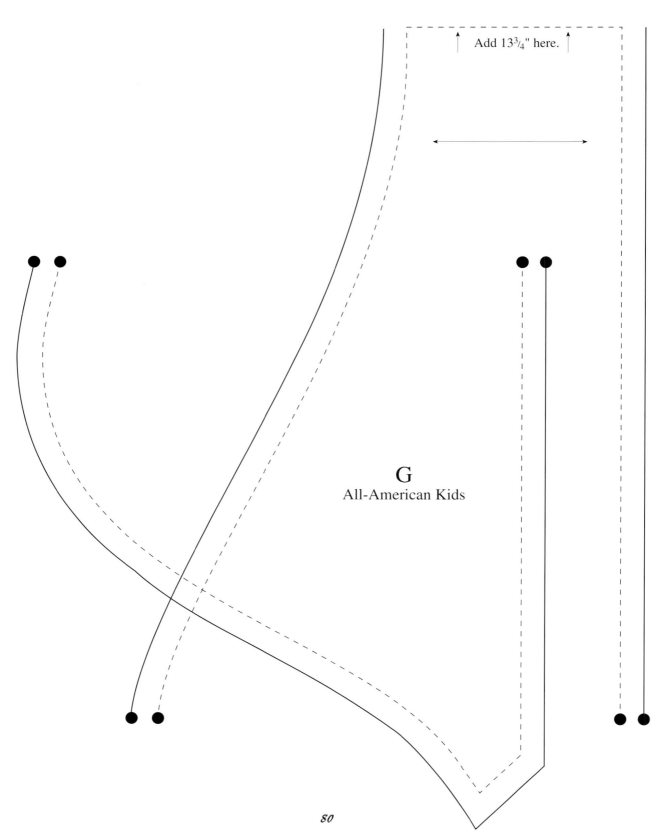

Add 13³/₄" here.

G
All-American Kids

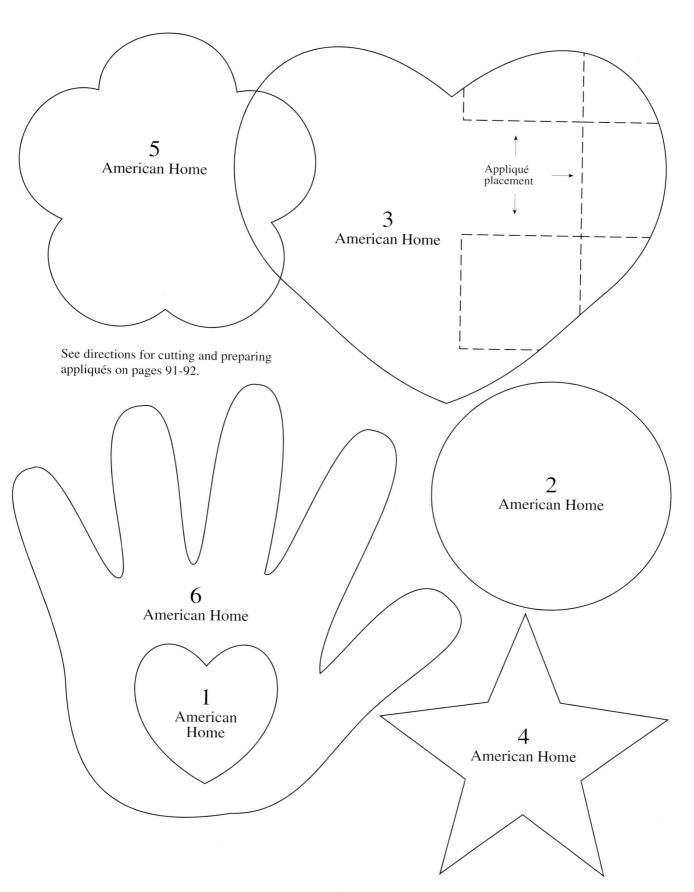

5
American Home

3
American Home

Appliqué
placement

See directions for cutting and preparing
appliqués on pages 91-92.

2
American Home

6
American Home

1
American
Home

4
American Home

Cats 'N Patches

Finished Size: 30$\frac{1}{2}$" x 39"
Finished Block Size: 12" x 12"

Materials (44"-wide fabric)	*Cutting* (Use templates on pages 86, 88 & 89.)
$\frac{1}{4}$ yd. blue for pieced sashing and pieced bottom border	8 pieces, each 2$\frac{1}{2}$" x 4" 29 squares, each 2$\frac{1}{2}$" x 2$\frac{1}{2}$"
$\frac{1}{4}$ yd. pale blue for pieced sashing and pieced bottom border	7 pieces, each 2$\frac{1}{2}$" x 4" 29 squares, each 2$\frac{1}{2}$" x 2$\frac{1}{2}$"
$\frac{1}{8}$ yd. purple for pieced bottom border	6 squares, each 2$\frac{7}{8}$" x 2$\frac{7}{8}$" See additional cutting information in directions for "Pieced Bottom Border" on page 84.
$\frac{1}{8}$ yd. light pink for pieced bottom border	6 squares, each 2$\frac{7}{8}$" x 2$\frac{7}{8}$" See additional cutting information in directions for "Pieced Bottom Border" on page 84.
$\frac{1}{2}$ yd. pale yellow fabric for pieced bottom border, appliqués, and cat block background and sashing	1 strip, 3$\frac{1}{2}$" x 30$\frac{1}{2}$" 2 strips, each 1$\frac{3}{4}$" x 10$\frac{1}{2}$" 2 strips, each 1$\frac{1}{2}$" x 12$\frac{1}{2}$" 1 piece, 4" x 4$\frac{1}{2}$" 2 pieces, each 2" x 3$\frac{1}{2}$" 1 piece, 2" x 4" 1 Template C 1 Template E 5 Star appliqués*
$\frac{1}{4}$ yd. lavender for cat block background and sashing	2 strips, each 1$\frac{3}{4}$" x 10$\frac{1}{2}$" 2 strips, each 1$\frac{1}{2}$" x 12$\frac{1}{2}$" 1 piece, 4" x 4$\frac{1}{2}$" 2 pieces, each 2" x 3$\frac{1}{2}$" 1 piece, 2" x 4" 1 Template C reversed 1 Template E reversed
$\frac{1}{8}$ yd. pink for appliqués	1 Heart 1 appliqué* 6 Heart 2 appliqués*

(continued on page 84)

Materials (continued)	**Cutting** (continued)
2 yds. white for paws, tails, alternate blocks, backing, and binding	1 piece, 35" x 43" for backing 2 squares, each 14½" x 14½" 4¼ yds. total of 2"-wide bias strips 1 Tail appliqué and 1 reversed* 8 Paw appliqués*
½ yd. brown for cat heads, ears and bodies	4 Template A 2 Template B See additional cutting information in directions for "Cat Blocks" on page 85.
½ yd. tan for bodies and necks	2 Template D and 2 Template D reversed See additional cutting information in directions for "Cat Blocks" on page 85.
35" x 43" piece of batting Four ¼"-diameter buttons for eyes White embroidery floss White thread for quilting	

*See directions for cutting and preparing appliqués on pages 91-92.

Directions

All seam allowances are ¼" wide.

Pieced Bottom Border

1. Sew the 2½" x 4" blue and pale blue rectangles together on the long edges in alternating fashion, starting with the darker blue. After adding the seventh rectangle (darker blue), add another darker blue one and continue alternating to complete the strip of 15 rectangles (Diagram 1).

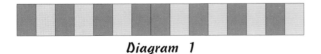

Diagram 1

2. Layer each purple 2⅞" square with a light pink square with right sides together. Cut diagonally, then stitch each resulting pair of triangles together along the long edge. Press the seam toward the purple triangle in each of the 12 resulting 2½" squares (Diagram 2).

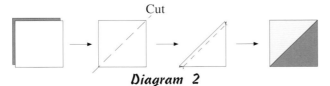

Diagram 2

3. Sew the squares together in sets of 3 squares each, making sure the pink triangle is always in the upper left position (Diagram 3).

Diagram 3

4. Sew the sets together as shown, adding 2½" squares of blue and pale blue where indicated in Diagram 4. Note that the second and fourth sets of squares are inverted so the purple triangle is in the upper left position.

Diagram 4

5. To assemble the pieced bottom border, sew the strip of squares to the top edge of the strip of blue rectangles. Then sew the 30½"-wide strip of yellow to the bottom edge (Diagram 5).

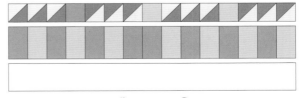

Diagram 5

6. Appliqué Heart 1 near the center of the strip (Diagram 6). See "Appliqué" on page 91 and refer to the quilt photo. Set aside.

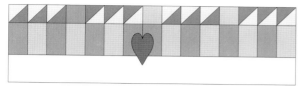

Diagram 6

Cat Blocks

1. Assemble 2 cat's heads, sewing the ears (Template A) and then the neck pieces (Template D) in place first. Add Template C last, stitching the long edge to the top of the head first, then stitching it to the ears in the directions of the arrows (Diagram 7).

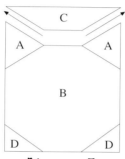

Diagram 7

Note: One cat's head will have a lavender Template C, the other a yellow one.

2. Using white embroidery floss, embroider the face on the upper left cat. Use the stem stitch for the mouth, backstitch for whiskers, and satin stitch for the nose. Sew buttons on for eyes (Diagram 8). Repeat for the cat on the lower right, reversing the design. Set aside.

Diagram 8

3. Assemble the body pieces. From the remaining tan and brown fabrics, cut 15"-long strips in widths from $^3/_4$" to $1^1/_4$". Sew the strips together, alternating the colors and widths to make a string-pieced unit that is at least 13" x 15" wide. From this unit, cut the following, making sure stripes are parallel with long edges: 2 pieces, each $3^1/_2$" x $5^1/_2$" for front legs; 2 pieces, each 4" x 5" for the bodies; and 1 of Template F and 1 of Template F reversed for the back legs (Diagram 9). Set aside.

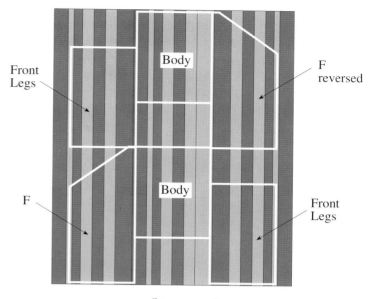

Diagram 9

4. Appliqué a tail to the yellow and lavender pieces cut from Template E, making sure that the lavender piece is reversed (Diagram 10). Appliqué a set of paws to the 2" x $3^1/_2$" yellow and lavender pieces.

Diagram 10

5. Assemble the cat blocks. Lay out the pieces for each block as shown, reversing the direction for the block with the lavender background. Sew the pieces together in vertical rows and press seams away from the striped sections in the legs and toward the background pieces in the center body section (Diagram 11).

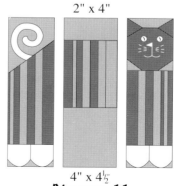

Diagram 11

6. Join the rows to complete each cat, then add the $1^3/_4$" x $10^1/_2$" strips to the sides of each body, adding yellow strips to the block with the lavender background, and lavender strips to the block with the yellow background. Then add matching $1^1/_2$" x $12^1/_2$" x strips to the top and bottom of each block (Diagram 12).

Diagram 12

Quilt Top Assembly

1. Appliqué Stars and Hearts 2 to the $14^1/_2$" white background squares, referring to the quilt photo for placement. Set aside.

2. Sew 3 blue and 3 pale blue $2^1/_2$" squares together for the top cat block, alternating the colors. Repeat. Sew the strips to the sides of the block. Sew 4 blue and 4 pale blue $2^1/_2$" squares together as shown. Sew strip to the top of the block (Diagram 13).

Diagram 13

3. Sew the $14^1/_2$" white background square to the right side of the top cat block, as shown in Diagram 14 on page 87.

4. Repeat for bottom cat block, sewing the 8-square strip to the bottom of the block as shown. Sew the remaining white background square to the left side of the block (Diagram 14 on page 87).

5. For the horizontal pieced sashing strip, join the remaining blue and pale blue $2^1/_2$" squares, alternating colors and beginning and ending with blue (Diagram 14 on page 87).

6. Sew the blocks, pieced sashing strip, and pieced bottom border together (Diagram 14 on page 87).

Cats 'N Patches

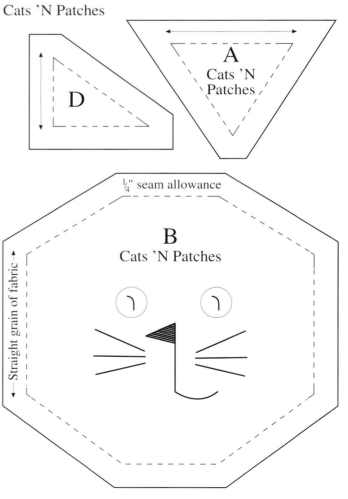

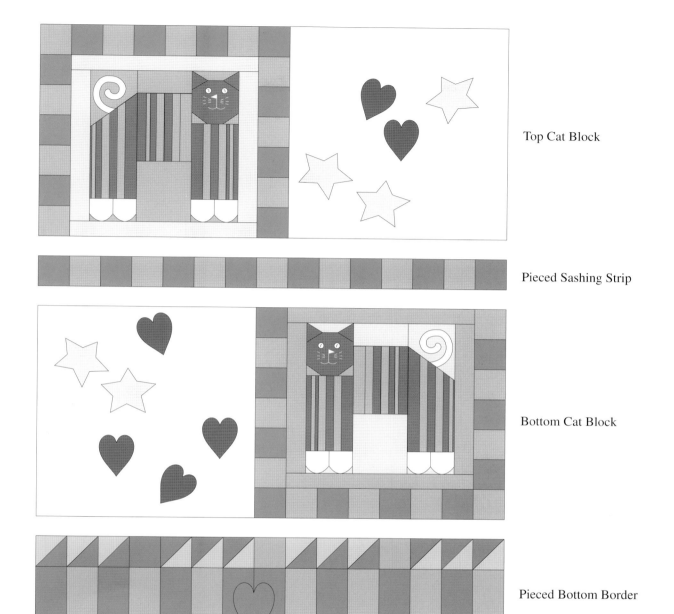

Top Cat Block

Pieced Sashing Strip

Bottom Cat Block

Pieced Bottom Border

Diagram 14

Finishing

Refer to pages 94-96 in the "General Directions."

1. Mark quilting lines as shown in Diagram 15 on page 88).

2. Layer the quilt top with batting and backing; baste.

3. Quilt by hand or machine, using white thread.

4. Bind the edges with double-layer white bias binding.

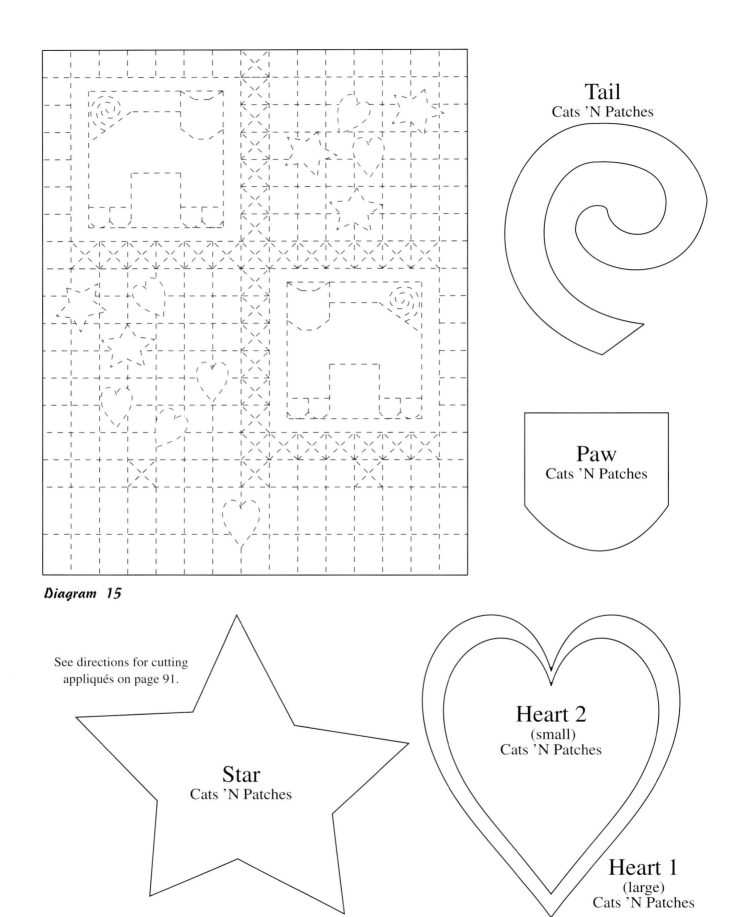

Diagram 15

Tail
Cats 'N Patches

Paw
Cats 'N Patches

See directions for cutting
appliqués on page 91.

Star
Cats 'N Patches

Heart 2
(small)
Cats 'N Patches

Heart 1
(large)
Cats 'N Patches

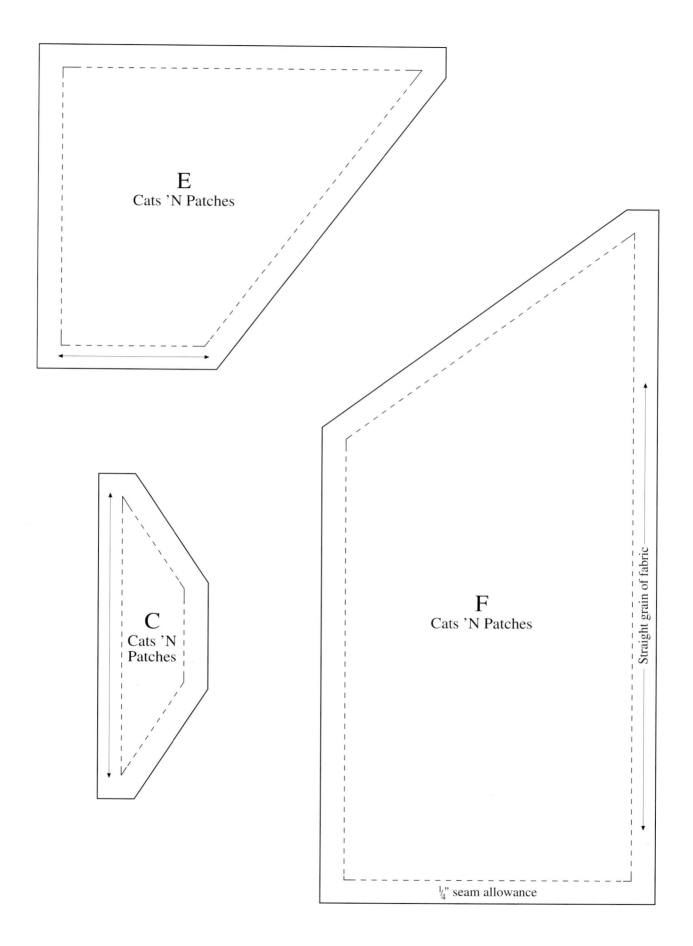

E
Cats 'N Patches

C
Cats 'N
Patches

F
Cats 'N Patches

Straight grain of fabric

¼" seam allowance

General Directions

The quilts in this book were made using several different techniques. Some blocks were pieced traditionally, using geometric fabric shapes. Some were string pieced, and some were appliquéd.

String Piecing

String piecing, used in combination with other fabric segments, is one of the quickest ways to create striking geometric designs. To string piece, first cut strips of fabric across the fabric width, from selvage to selvage. Then sew the strips right sides together, stitching 1/4" from the matching raw edges. Press all seams in each string-pieced unit in one direction, unless the specific quilt instructions say otherwise. Then cut the string unit into the desired shapes using templates, scissors or a rotary cutter, ruler, and mat.

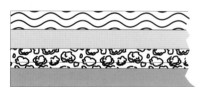

Sew strips together.   Cut into desired shape.

Making Templates

Full-size cutting templates are provided for the quilts in this book. Make these from template plastic or cardboard. Block piecing templates include 1/4"-wide seam allowances. Appliqué templates do not always include seam allowances.

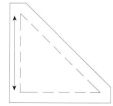

Piecing Template   Appliqué Template
(no seam allowances)

To make plastic templates for piecing, place the template material on top of each template required for your quilt. Using an indelible pen, carefully trace the cutting and stitching lines and the grain line arrows. Label each piece with the pattern name and letter. Cut out along the outer lines.

To make cardboard templates, first trace the template onto graph paper. Mount the graph paper onto cardboard and cut out each template along the outer lines. Mark each template as described above.

To make appliqué templates, trace around the template and cut out on the marked line. Label as described above.

Fabric Preparation, Marking, and Cutting

Before you mark and cut the pieces required for your quilt, wash, dry, and press all fabric.

Quiltmakers usually cut all pieces for a quilt before they begin to piece. However, with the more complex quilts in this book, the cutting instructions are sometimes given one block at a time to avoid confusing pieces that are similar. It's a good idea to carefully label each set of pieces to avoid confusion later.

To mark around templates on light-colored fabrics, use a sharp #2 lead pencil. On dark-colored fabrics, use a sharp, white dressmaker's pencil, a sliver of soap, or a silver or yellow fabric marking pencil. Chalk pencils or chalk-wheel markers also make clear marks on fabric. Be sure to test whatever tool you decide to use on your fabric first, to make sure the marks can be removed easily.

Lay out the templates to make the best use of the fabric, making sure to position the grain-line on each parallel to the lengthwise or crosswise grain of the fabric. It is a good idea to cut the larger pieces first—border and sashing strips for example—before cutting the smaller template pieces.

Mark piecing templates on the wrong side of the fabric and cut them out on the outer solid line, using sharp scissors or a rotary cutter, ruler and mat.

Mark appliqué templates on the right side of the fabric. Cut out appliqué shapes, using sharp scissors and adding a scant ¼" allowance all around, unless the template you are using has seam allowances included (indicated by a dashed line).

Piecing the Blocks

The most important thing to remember about piecing is to maintain a consistent ¼"-wide seam allowance throughout. Otherwise, the quilt blocks will not be the desired finished size. Measurements for all components of each quilt are based on blocks that finish accurately to the desired size plus ¼" on each edge for seam allowances.

Take the time to establish an exact ¼"-wide seam guide on your machine. Some machines have a special quilting foot designed so that the right-hand and left-hand edges of the foot measure exactly ¼" from the center needle position. This allows you to use the edge of the presser foot to guide the cut edge of the fabric for a perfect ¼"-wide seam allowance.

If your machine doesn't have such a foot, you can create a seam guide so it will be easy to stitch an accurate ¼"-wide seam allowance.

1. Place a ruler or piece of graph paper with four squares to the inch under your presser foot.

2. Gently lower the needle onto the first ¼" line from the right edge of the ruler or paper. Place several layers of masking tape or a narrow strip of moleskin (available in drug stores) along the right-hand edge of the ruler or paper, so that it does not interfere with the feed dog. Test your new guide to make sure your seams are ¼" wide; if not, readjust your guide.

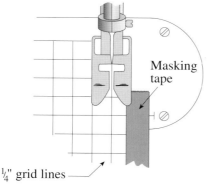

Masking tape

¼" grid lines

If possible, chain piece to speed up your work. To chain piece, sew the seam to join two pieces, Then, without lifting the presser foot or removing the first set of pieces, feed the next set of pieces into the machine and continue stitching. Continue feeding pieces through the machine without cutting the threads in between. When all the pieces have been sewn, remove the chain of pieces from the machine and clip the threads between them.

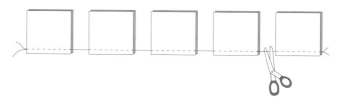

Pressing

The traditional rule in quiltmaking is to press seams to one side, toward the darker color whenever possible. First, press the seam flat as stitched from the wrong side, then press the seam in the desired direction from the right side. Press carefully to avoid distorting the shapes.

When joining two seamed units, it is usually possible to plan ahead and press the seam allowances in opposite directions as shown. This reduces bulk and makes it easier to match seam lines. Where two seams meet, the seam allowances will butt up against each other, making it easier to join units with perfectly matched seam intersections.

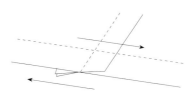

Press opposing seams in opposite directions before joining.

Appliqué

Appliqué is used to add details to quilts and to create curved designs that are more difficult to create with piecing. Some of the quilts in this book have pieces appliquéd on top of the pieced blocks, in quilt background areas, or to create designs for alternate blocks between the string-pieced ones.

There are many ways to appliqué. One of the easiest is to carefully turn under the marked seam allowance on each piece, rolling the traced line just to the underside of the appliqué so it won't show. Then baste the turned edge in place, keeping the stitches near the fold. Do not turn under edges that will be covered by other appliqué pieces. They should lie flat under the appliqué piece that will lie on top. Clip the seam allowance almost to the marked line on curves and points (like those on hearts and stars) so that you can turn the edge under easily.

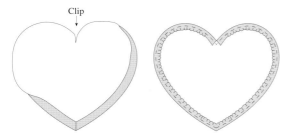

Pin or baste the appliqué pieces in place on the background fabric or block, then use a blind stitch to sew the shapes in place. Be sure to use thread that matches the color of the appliqué.

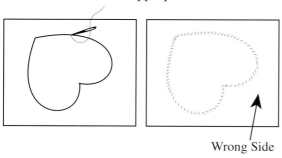

Wrong Side

When stitching inside points where you have clipped in order to turn under the edge, make stitches smaller as you sew within $1/_2$" of the point. Stitch past the point, then return to the point to add one extra stitch to emphasize the point. Come up through the appliqué, catching a little more fabric in the inside point (four or five threads instead of one or two). Make a straight stitch outward, going under the point to pull it in a little and emphasize the shape of the point.

If your inside point frays, use a few close stitches to tack the fabric down securely. If your thread matches your appliqué fabric, these stitches will blend in with the edge of the shape.

Piecing the Quilt Top

It's a good idea to measure each block after pressing to make sure it is square and then make any necessary adjustments. Be sure to press the border and sashing strips to remove creases and wrinkles before you sew the quilt top together.

Most quilts are constructed in either horizontal or vertical rows. Sometimes the blocks in each row have sashing strips between them, as well as above and below them. Follow the assembly diagram for the quilt you are making to lay out and sew the blocks together in the required rows. Then sew the rows together in the correct order to complete the quilt top. Be careful to match block seam lines where they meet if the rows are not separated by sashing.

Adding Borders

Borders frame the quilt. Some quilts have no borders, relying on a narrow contrasting binding around the outer edges to create the frame. Others have wider strips of fabric beyond the blocks.

Cutting directions are given for the border strips for the quilts in this book. However, it's a good idea to wait to cut the borders until after you have completed the quilt top and then measure the top.

The edges of a quilt often measure slightly longer than the distance through the quilt center due to stretching during construction. Sometimes, each edge is a different length.

Measure the quilt top through the center in both directions to determine how long to cut the border strips. This step ensures that the finished quilt will be as straight and as "square" as possible, without wavy edges. How you measure depends on whether the quilt has straight-cut or mitered corners. To measure and add borders with straight-cut corners:

1. Measure the length of the quilt top through the center. Cut border strips to that measurement, piecing as necessary; mark the centers of the quilt top and the border strips.

   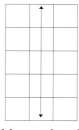

   Measure length at center.

   Pin the borders to the sides of the quilt top, matching the centers and

92

ends and easing if necessary. Sew the border strips in place. Press the seams toward the border.

Press seams
toward borders.

2. Measure the width of the quilt through the center, including the side borders just added. Cut border strips to that measurement, piecing as necessary; mark the center of the quilt top and the border strips. Pin the borders to the top and bottom of the quilt top, matching the center marks and ends and easing as necessary. Sew the border strips in place. Press the seams toward the border.

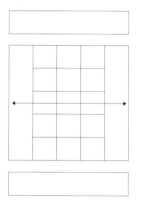
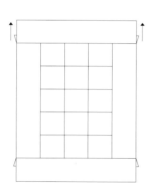

Measure width at
center after adding
side borders.

To measure and add borders with mitered corners:

1. First measure through the quilt center in both the lengthwise and crosswise directions and add to these measurements the width of the borders. Border strips should be cut to this length plus at least ¹/₂" for seam allowances; it's safer to add 2"-3" to give yourself some leeway.

2. Mark the center of the quilt edges and the centers of the border strips. Stitch the borders to the quilt with a ¹/₄"-wide seam, matching the centers; the border strips should extend the same distance at each end of the quilt. Start and stop your stitching ¹/₄" from the corners of the quilt; press the seams toward the borders.

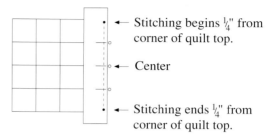

← Stitching begins ¹/₄" from corner of quilt top.

← Center

← Stitching ends ¹/₄" from corner of quilt top.

3. Lay the first corner to be mitered on the ironing board. Fold under one strip at a 45-degree angle and adjust so seam lines match perfectly. Press and pin securely.

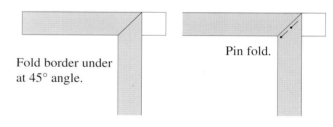

Fold border under at 45° angle.

Pin fold.

4. Fold the quilt diagonally with right sides together, lining up the edges of the border. If necessary, use a ruler to draw a pencil line on the crease to make the line more visible. Stitch on the pressed crease, sewing from the corner to the outside edge. Press the seam open and trim away excess border strip, leaving a ¹/₄"-wide seam allowance.

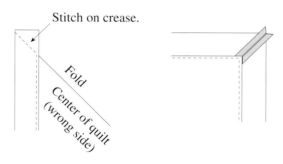

Stitch on crease.

Fold
Center of quilt
(wrong side)

5. Repeat with the remaining corners.

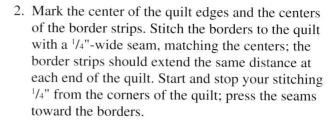

Preparing the Quilt

After piecing the blocks together and adding the borders, it's time to turn the quilt top into a quilt by adding a batting and a backing and quilting the layers together. Quilting turns an ordinary quilt into a masterpiece, adding texture, beauty, and durability to your work. Quilting suggestions are included with each of the quilt patterns in this book.

Before you layer your completed quilt top with the batting and backing, mark the quilting lines on the freshly pressed quilt top. Marking is not necessary if you plan to quilt "in the ditch," or outline quilt a uniform distance from the seam lines. Mark more complex quilt designs on the quilt top *before* the quilt is layered with batting and backing.

Choose a marking tool that will be visible on your fabric, and test it on fabric scraps to be sure the marks can be removed easily. Masking tape can also be used to mark straight quilting. Tape only small sections at a time and remove the tape when you stop at the end of the day; otherwise, the sticky residue may be difficult to remove from the fabric.

Backing and Batting

Cut the quilt backing so that it extends 2" to 4" beyond the outer edges of the quilt. For large quilts, it is usually necessary to sew two or three lengths of fabric together to make a backing of the required size. Press the backing seams open to make quilting easier.

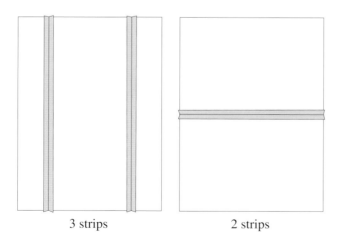

3 strips   2 strips

Batting comes packaged in standard bed sizes, or it can be purchased by the yard. Several weights or thicknesses are available. Thick battings are fine for tied quilts and comforters; a thinner batting is better, however, if you intend to quilt by hand or machine.

Unroll the batting and let it relax overnight before you layer your quilt. Some batting may need to be pre-washed, while other types should definitely not be pre-washed; be sure to check the manufacturer's package instructions.

Layering the Quilt

After preparing the batting and backing and pressing the completed quilt top, create a quilt sandwich with the three layers.

1. Spread the backing, wrong side up, on a flat, clean surface. Anchor it with pins or masking tape. Be careful not to stretch the backing out of shape.

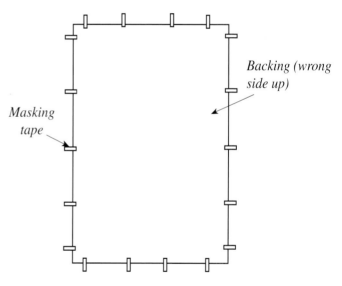

Backing (wrong side up)

Masking tape

2. Cut the batting the same size as the backing. Spread it out on top of backing, smoothing out any wrinkles.

3. Place the pressed quilt to on top of the batting. Smooth out any wrinkles. Make sure the edges of the quilt top are parallel to the edges of the backing.

4. Baste with needle and thread, starting in the center and working diagonally to each corner. Continue basting, in a grid of horizontal and vertical lines 6"-8" apart. Finish by basting around the edges.

Note: For machine quilting you may baste the layers with #2 rustproof safety pins. Place pins about 6"-8" apart, away from the area you intend to quilt.

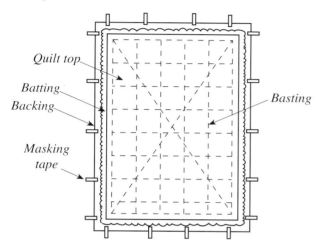

Quilt top

Batting

Backing

Basting

Masking tape

5. Use your favorite method—hand or machine quilting—to quilt your quilt. Remove the basting.

Binding

After the quilting is completed, finish the edges with a binding in a matching or contrasting color. First trim the backing and batting to match the outer edge of the quilt top.

The quilts in this book were finished with binding cut on the true bias of the fabric and finish to a width of 1/4". For a wall hanging, a single-layer binding is adequate. On larger quilts, a double-layer binding was used for added durability. The appropriate width and length for binding strips is included in the cutting directions for each quilt. If you wish to finish your quilts with a wider binding, adjust the cut width of the strip and the seam allowance accordingly. (You may need more fabric if you do so.)

To attach binding:

1. Sew the bias strips, right sides together, to make one long piece of binding. Press seams open.

2. For double-layer binding only, fold the strip in half lengthwise, wrong sides together, and press.

Wrong side

Right side

3. At one end of the bias strip, turn under 1/4" at a 45-degree angle. Press. (Illustrations below show double-layer binding.)

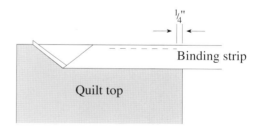

Fold line

4. Starting on one side of the quilt, stitch the binding to the quilt, using a 1/4"-wide seam allowance. End the stitching 1/4" from the corner of the quilt and backstitch.

1/4"

Binding strip

Quilt top

5. Turn the quilt so that you will be stitching down the next side. Fold the binding up away from the quilt.

Quilt top

6. Fold binding back down onto itself parallel with the edge of the quilt top. Begin stitching at the edge, backstitching to secure.

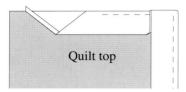

7. Repeat on the remaining edges and corners of the quilt. When you reach the beginning of the binding, overlap the beginning stitches by about 1" and cut away any excess binding, trimming the end at a 45-degree angle. Tuck the end of the binding into the fold and finish the seam.

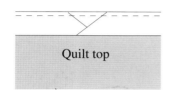

8. Fold the binding over the raw edges of the quilt to the back and blindstitch in place with the folded edge covering the row of machine stitching. A miter will form at each corner. Blindstitch the mitered corners in place.

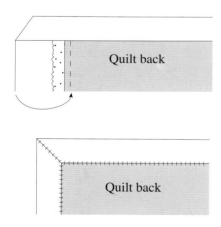

Adding a Hanging Sleeve

If you plan to hang your quilt on the wall, add a hanging sleeve to hold a curtain rod or wooden dowel.

1. Using leftover fabric from the front or a piece of muslin, cut a strip 6" wide and 1" shorter than the width of the quilt at the top edge. Fold the ends under ¹/₂", then ¹/₂" again, and stitch.

2. Fold the fabric strip in half lengthwise, *wrong sides together*, and stitch ¹/₄" from the edges. Press the seam open, centering it in the tube you have created.

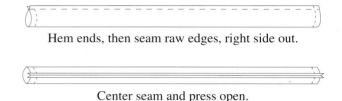

Hem ends, then seam raw edges, right side out.

Center seam and press open.

3. Position the tube just below the inner edge of the binding with the seam against the backing. Blindstitch the top edge of the tube to the quilt, then scoot the top up a little before blindstitching the bottom edge in place. This adds a little give to the sleeve so the hanging rod doesn't strain the quilt.

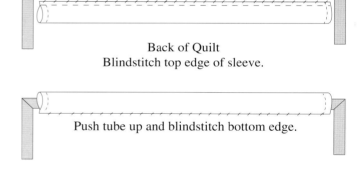

Back of Quilt
Blindstitch top edge of sleeve.

Push tube up and blindstitch bottom edge.

Adding the Finishing Touch

Signing and dating your masterpiece not only enhances its meaning, but also adds to its value for future generations. One way to do this is to write your name and date on a piece of muslin or other light-colored fabric using an indelible pen. Then turn under the raw edges neatly and slipstitch the label to the back of the quilt. If you wish, you can embroider or cross-stitch a special label for your quilt. Be sure to add the name of the quilt, the location where it was made, and any other information that might interest future generations.